Direct Listings and Non-Traditional Public Offerings

How Companies Go Public Without Traditional IPO Underwriting

By Joe Correa

Published by Live Stronger Faster

This book is for educational and informational purposes only. The author and publisher are not engaged in rendering legal, financial, or other professional advice. Readers should consult a qualified professional before making any financial decisions.

First Edition

Table of Contents

Introduction 5

Chapter 1: Understanding Direct Listings and the Evolution of Modern Public Offerings.. 15

Chapter 2: Comparing Traditional IPOs vs. Direct Listings... 34

Chapter 3: The Mechanics of a Direct Listing........................ 53

Chapter 4: Advantages and Disadvantages of Direct Listings 72

Chapter 5: Pricing, Valuation, and Market Dynamics in Direct Listings... 92

Chapter 6: Investor Psychology and Market Perception in Direct Listings.. 111

Chapter 7: Regulatory Requirements and Exchange Rules for Direct Listings.. 130

Chapter 8: Building a Company That Is Ready for a Direct Listing..148

Chapter 9: Liquidity, Founder Wealth, and Employee Equity in Direct Listings.. 166

Chapter 10: The Future of Direct Listings and the Evolution of Public Markets...184

Final IPO Thoughts...203

Introduction

The world of public markets is evolving rapidly, and entrepreneurs today have more ways than ever before to bring their companies to the public stage. For decades, the traditional initial public offering, commonly known as the IPO, dominated the financial headlines as the primary method companies used to become publicly traded. Businesses hired major investment banks, roadshows were organized across financial centers, institutional investors received privileged access to shares, and underwriters controlled much of the process. While this traditional pathway created some of the largest and most successful public companies in history, it was not always the perfect fit for every business. Over time, innovative alternatives emerged that allowed companies to bypass many of the restrictions, costs, delays, and complexities associated with traditional underwriting structures.

This book explores one of the most fascinating and rapidly growing developments in modern capital markets: direct listings and non-traditional public offerings. These alternative methods have changed how founders, investors, employees, and private companies think about liquidity, ownership, fundraising, valuation, and long-term wealth creation. Instead of following the conventional IPO model, companies now have multiple options available to enter the public markets while maintaining greater flexibility, transparency, and control.

The rise of direct listings has opened an entirely new chapter in corporate finance. Businesses such as Spotify, Slack, and Coinbase demonstrated that companies could achieve public market access without relying on traditional underwriting syndicates in the same way previous generations had. These landmark transactions challenged decades of Wall Street norms and proved that innovative companies with strong brands, substantial private investor demand, and solid financial foundations could approach public offerings differently.

For entrepreneurs, this shift represents much more than a technical financial change. It represents freedom. It creates opportunities for founders to maintain greater ownership, reduce dilution, improve pricing transparency, and potentially avoid some of the costly inefficiencies associated with traditional IPOs. For investors, it provides new ways to evaluate businesses entering the market. For employees holding equity compensation, it can create earlier liquidity opportunities and more efficient access to the value they helped create. For the financial industry as a whole, it reflects the growing democratization of capital markets and the increasing power of technology-driven businesses to challenge traditional systems. Understanding direct listings and non-traditional offerings requires more than simply learning definitions. It requires understanding the evolution of public markets themselves. Historically, investment banks served as gatekeepers that controlled access to institutional capital and public exchanges. Underwriters determined offering prices, allocated shares to select investors, stabilized stock prices after listing, and managed the marketing process. While these services created significant benefits for certain companies, they also introduced high fees, pricing inefficiencies, and concerns about fairness. Many founders began questioning whether traditional underwriting truly aligned with their long-term interests.

One of the most controversial aspects of traditional IPOs has been underpricing. Numerous companies experienced massive stock price increases on their first trading day after going public. While media headlines celebrated these "IPO pops," many founders and executives recognized that dramatic first-day gains often meant their companies sold shares below true market value. In other words, the company may have left enormous amounts of money on the table. Billions of dollars in potential company value sometimes transferred immediately to institutional investors who received preferred share allocations before the stock began trading publicly.

Direct listings emerged as an alternative solution to some of these challenges. Instead of issuing new shares through an underwriting syndicate, companies could allow existing shareholders to sell shares directly into the open market. Market-driven supply and demand would determine pricing rather than pre-negotiated underwriting structures. This approach could reduce dilution, eliminate many underwriting fees, and improve transparency in the price discovery process. At the same time, it introduced new risks and operational considerations that founders and executives needed to understand carefully.

The financial world continues to innovate far beyond direct listings alone. Modern companies now evaluate a broad spectrum of public market pathways, including reverse mergers, SPAC mergers, hybrid offerings, auction-based systems, Regulation A+ offerings, direct public offerings, dual-class share structures, cross-border listings, decentralized finance-based fundraising mechanisms, and secondary market liquidity solutions. The capital markets landscape is no longer defined by a single formula. Companies must now strategically analyze which path best aligns with their business model, growth stage, shareholder structure, capital requirements, and long-term vision.

This transformation has become especially important for technology companies, creator-driven businesses, platform companies, software firms, AI businesses, fintech startups, and globally scalable digital enterprises. Many modern businesses achieve massive scale before ever considering a public listing. Venture capital funding, private equity, secondary markets, and global investor networks allow companies to remain private much longer than previous generations. As a result, by the time some businesses consider entering public markets, they may already possess strong brand awareness, millions of users, stable revenue, and extensive private investor demand. These conditions create opportunities for alternative listing structures that may not have existed decades ago.

For founders, one of the greatest advantages of understanding non-traditional public offerings is strategic flexibility. Every company is unique. Some businesses need immediate capital raises to fuel expansion. Others prioritize liquidity for early investors and employees. Some founders want to maintain voting control through dual-class shares. Others seek maximum transparency and broad retail participation. Some companies require the marketing support and analyst coverage provided by traditional underwriters, while others already possess global recognition and strong customer communities that reduce dependence on Wall Street promotion.

This book is designed to help readers understand not only how direct listings work mechanically, but also why they matter strategically. Public offerings are not simply financial transactions. They are life-changing wealth events that can dramatically alter the future of founders, employees, investors, and entire industries. The decisions made before, during, and after a public offering can influence ownership control, long-term valuation, personal wealth, tax obligations, investor relationships, media perception, and corporate governance for decades.

One of the most important concepts throughout this book is alignment. Successful public market transitions occur when a company's structure aligns with its objectives. A founder pursuing maximum long-term control may choose a different path than a founder prioritizing rapid liquidity. A highly profitable technology company with strong cash reserves may approach public markets differently than a capital-intensive manufacturing company that requires large fundraising rounds. Businesses with substantial retail consumer brands may benefit from public participation strategies differently than enterprise-focused companies operating behind the scenes.

Another major theme explored throughout this book is the balance between liquidity and control. Going public creates opportunities for wealth creation, but it also introduces new responsibilities and pressures. Public companies operate under increased regulatory scrutiny, quarterly reporting expectations, investor relations demands, governance requirements, and market volatility. Founders who once maintained near-total operational freedom may suddenly face pressure from analysts, institutional shareholders, activist investors, and public market expectations. Understanding these trade-offs before entering public markets is essential.

Many entrepreneurs become fascinated with valuations and headlines while overlooking the operational realities of being public. However, sustainable wealth creation requires much more than achieving a successful listing. It requires building a durable business capable of thriving under public market conditions. Investors ultimately reward companies that demonstrate strong execution, scalable systems, predictable financial performance, effective leadership, and long-term strategic discipline. A public listing is not the finish line. In many ways, it is only the beginning of an entirely new phase of corporate growth.

This book also examines how non-traditional offerings are reshaping access to investment opportunities. Historically, many of the greatest wealth-building opportunities occurred before companies became publicly traded. Retail investors often gained access only after significant value appreciation had already occurred. As financial technology evolves and regulatory frameworks adapt, broader participation models may continue emerging that allow public investors earlier access to growth-stage companies. Understanding these trends can help both founders and investors prepare for the future evolution of capital markets.

The growth of decentralized finance, blockchain technology, tokenization, and digital securities may eventually transform public offerings even further. Financial systems continue becoming more global, digital, and accessible. While traditional stock exchanges remain central pillars of modern finance, innovation continues accelerating. Future public offerings may involve hybrid models that combine traditional regulation with blockchain-based infrastructure, global liquidity pools, smart contracts, and decentralized ownership frameworks. Entrepreneurs who understand these shifts early may position themselves advantageously for future opportunities.

Throughout this book, readers will explore the mechanics, advantages, disadvantages, risks, regulations, strategic considerations, and long-term implications of direct listings and non-traditional public offerings. You will learn how companies prepare for these transactions, how pricing mechanisms work, how exchanges evaluate listing eligibility, how investor relations strategies evolve, and how founders can position themselves for long-term wealth creation rather than short-term hype. You will also discover that successful public offerings are deeply connected to broader business fundamentals. Strong financial controls, transparent reporting systems, scalable operations, effective leadership teams, strategic legal structures, investor communication frameworks, and sustainable revenue growth remain essential regardless of which listing pathway a company chooses. Alternative public offering structures do not eliminate the need for disciplined execution. Instead, they provide different tools that companies can use strategically depending on their unique circumstances.

The entrepreneurs who benefit most from these evolving opportunities are often those who think long term. They understand that wealth creation is not simply about achieving liquidity as quickly as possible. It is about building enduring value over decades. Public markets can become extraordinary engines for wealth creation when approached strategically. Equity ownership, appreciation, secondary offerings, acquisitions, strategic partnerships, stock-based compensation, and long-term capital allocation can all contribute to exponential financial growth when managed wisely.

At its core, this book is about empowerment. It is about helping entrepreneurs, executives, investors, and ambitious professionals understand that there is no longer only one path to accessing public capital markets. Innovation has expanded the possibilities. Companies now have greater ability to design listing strategies that align with their missions, cultures, ownership structures, and long-term goals. Founders can think more creatively about how to balance growth, control, liquidity, and wealth preservation in ways previous generations could not.

The future of capital markets will likely continue evolving faster than many people expect. Technology, regulation, globalization, investor behavior, and financial innovation are reshaping how businesses raise capital and create wealth. The entrepreneurs who understand these shifts will be better positioned to build companies that thrive not only privately, but also publicly. They will be able to evaluate opportunities more intelligently, negotiate from stronger positions, and make strategic decisions that maximize long-term enterprise value.

As you move through this book, remember that direct listings and alternative public offerings are not merely financial tools. They are strategic frameworks capable of transforming personal wealth, business growth, ownership dynamics, and generational financial outcomes. The companies that master these strategies may redefine entire industries while creating extraordinary opportunities for founders, employees, investors, and future entrepreneurs around the world.

Welcome to the next evolution of public markets, founder wealth creation, and modern capital markets strategy.

Chapter 1

Understanding Direct Listings and the Evolution of Modern Public Offerings

The history of public markets is deeply connected to the evolution of capitalism, entrepreneurship, and wealth creation itself. For generations, businesses seeking large amounts of capital eventually turned toward public stock exchanges to raise money, expand operations, reward investors, and create liquidity opportunities for founders and employees. Traditional initial public offerings, commonly known as IPOs, became the standard method companies used to transition from private ownership into publicly traded corporations. Investment banks organized the process, institutional investors received early allocations, and stock exchanges became the center of global financial activity. Yet over time, entrepreneurs and financial innovators began questioning whether the traditional IPO system truly represented the most efficient and founder-friendly pathway to becoming a public company.

Direct listings emerged from this growing desire for flexibility, transparency, efficiency, and control. Unlike traditional IPOs, direct listings allow companies to become publicly traded without relying on the conventional underwriting structure that has dominated Wall Street for decades. Instead of issuing newly created shares through investment banks that pre-price and distribute the offering to selected institutional investors, a direct listing allows existing shareholders to sell their shares directly on a public exchange once trading begins. This seemingly simple difference fundamentally changes the economics, incentives, and dynamics of going public.

To understand why direct listings became important, it is essential to first understand the limitations and criticisms associated with traditional IPOs. Historically, investment banks played a central role in public offerings because they provided expertise, credibility, institutional investor access, regulatory guidance, and marketing support. Underwriters conducted roadshows, built investor demand, helped determine offering prices, stabilized trading after launch, and coordinated the entire public transition process. In exchange, these banks earned significant underwriting fees that could amount to tens or even hundreds of millions of dollars for large transactions.

For many companies, these services were valuable and necessary. However, over time, founders and executives began noticing several recurring problems. One of the largest concerns involved IPO underpricing. Numerous companies experienced massive stock price increases on their first day of trading. While media outlets celebrated these dramatic gains as signs of successful offerings, many executives saw the situation differently. If a company's stock surged 40%, 60%, or even 100% on the first day, it often meant the company had sold shares far below what the market was actually willing to pay. In practical terms, billions of dollars in potential company value may have been transferred immediately to favored institutional investors rather than remaining with the company or its original shareholders.

This realization created frustration among founders who spent years building their businesses only to watch substantial value shift away during the public offering process. Critics argued that traditional IPO systems sometimes prioritized the interests of investment banks and institutional clients over the interests of the companies themselves. Founders began asking difficult questions. Why should underwriters determine pricing behind closed doors? Why should select institutional investors receive preferential allocations? Why should companies pay enormous underwriting fees if they already possessed strong brand awareness and investor demand?

The rise of technology companies accelerated these questions even further. Modern technology businesses often achieved global recognition before ever considering a public offering. Platforms with millions of users, powerful network effects, strong revenues, and extensive private investor backing no longer depended on Wall Street promotion in the same way earlier industrial companies once did. Some businesses already possessed enormous visibility, loyal customer bases, and strong investor interest long before listing publicly. As a result, alternative pathways to public markets became increasingly realistic.

One of the most influential moments in the rise of direct listings occurred when Spotify chose to go public through a direct listing rather than a traditional IPO. The company's decision attracted enormous global attention because it challenged decades of established financial norms. Spotify argued that its globally recognized brand, large user base, and extensive existing shareholder network reduced the need for a traditional underwriting process. Rather than raising new capital through newly issued shares, Spotify allowed existing shareholders to sell directly into the market once trading opened.

This approach created several important differences compared to traditional IPO structures. First, direct listings generally avoided the lock-up periods commonly imposed in traditional IPOs. In many IPOs, insiders and early investors are restricted from selling shares for several months after the offering. Direct listings often provide more immediate liquidity opportunities for existing shareholders. Second, direct listings can reduce underwriting fees substantially because investment banks play a more limited advisory role rather than fully underwriting the transaction. Third, direct listings allow market-driven supply and demand to determine the opening stock price more naturally rather than relying heavily on pre-negotiated pricing.

However, direct listings also introduced new risks and complexities. Without traditional underwriting stabilization mechanisms, stock prices could become more volatile during early trading. Companies also needed sufficient market recognition and investor demand to generate trading liquidity successfully. Additionally, direct listings historically did not raise new capital directly for the company, although regulatory developments later created more flexibility around primary share issuance in certain direct listing structures.

The evolution of non-traditional public offerings reflects broader changes occurring throughout global financial systems. Technology continues reducing barriers between businesses and investors. Information flows more rapidly than ever before. Retail investors possess increasing access to financial markets through digital trading platforms. Private capital markets have expanded dramatically, allowing companies to remain private longer while still raising enormous amounts of funding. As these trends continue, companies now possess far greater flexibility when evaluating how and when to access public markets. Another important factor driving alternative public offerings is the changing relationship between founders and ownership control. Many entrepreneurs today prioritize maintaining long-term strategic influence over their companies even after going public. Traditional public offerings can create pressure from institutional investors focused heavily on short-term quarterly performance. Alternative structures sometimes provide founders with greater flexibility regarding voting rights, share structures, governance arrangements, and liquidity timing.

This shift became especially important within industries driven by innovation, long-term research, and rapid technological change. Founders leading transformative businesses often believe their visions require patience and strategic continuity that may conflict with short-term market expectations. As a result, companies increasingly explore structures that allow access to public capital while preserving founder influence and long-term operational flexibility.

The rise of direct listings also reflects the growing sophistication of modern private markets. Venture capital firms, private equity funds, secondary marketplaces, family offices, sovereign wealth funds, and institutional investors now provide extensive private funding options long before businesses consider public listings. Some companies raise billions of dollars privately while achieving valuations previously seen only in public markets. Because of this evolution, many businesses no longer require traditional IPO capital infusions as urgently as earlier generations did.

Instead, some companies pursue public listings primarily to create liquidity opportunities for employees, founders, and early investors rather than to raise new operating capital. Direct listings can align particularly well with this objective because they focus more heavily on enabling existing shareholders to sell shares into public markets rather than issuing large amounts of new stock. This distinction may help reduce dilution while creating more flexible liquidity pathways.

The psychology surrounding public offerings has also evolved significantly. Historically, IPOs often represented prestige milestones associated with corporate maturity and legitimacy. Today, founders increasingly view public listings as strategic financial tools rather than purely symbolic achievements. Entrepreneurs now ask more detailed questions about timing, ownership dilution, regulatory burden, investor expectations, and long-term wealth outcomes before deciding how to structure public transactions.

At the same time, regulatory agencies and stock exchanges continue adapting to financial innovation. Exchanges such as the New York Stock Exchange and NASDAQ have worked to develop frameworks supporting alternative listing methods while maintaining investor protections and market integrity. Regulatory adjustments surrounding direct listings, SPACs, and hybrid structures demonstrate how rapidly the public market ecosystem continues evolving.

Despite the excitement surrounding alternative offerings, it is important to recognize that direct listings are not automatically superior to traditional IPOs. Every company possesses unique circumstances, goals, financial conditions, shareholder structures, and strategic priorities. Some businesses still benefit greatly from traditional underwriting support, especially companies requiring substantial capital raises, extensive institutional marketing, or post-listing stabilization. Others may prefer hybrid approaches combining elements of multiple offering structures.

The most successful public market strategies begin with alignment between the company's objectives and its chosen pathway. Founders must carefully evaluate whether they prioritize capital raising, liquidity, ownership preservation, pricing efficiency, brand visibility, investor diversification, governance flexibility, or long-term strategic independence.

No single structure fits every business. Understanding the advantages and disadvantages of each pathway is essential for making informed decisions. One of the greatest misconceptions about going public is the belief that listing on a stock exchange automatically creates sustainable wealth. In reality, long-term wealth creation depends far more on business fundamentals than on the specific listing mechanism used. Public markets reward companies that execute effectively, scale efficiently, maintain strong governance, communicate transparently, and deliver sustainable long-term growth. A successful listing creates opportunity, but lasting value depends on operational performance over time.

Founders must also prepare for the emotional and psychological realities of becoming public. Private companies often operate with substantial confidentiality and flexibility. Public companies face constant scrutiny from analysts, investors, regulators, media organizations, competitors, and shareholders. Quarterly earnings reports, stock price volatility, public criticism, activist investors, and governance pressures can dramatically alter the operating environment for executives and founders.

Understanding these realities before entering public markets is critical. Many founders spend years obsessing over achieving liquidity events while underestimating the operational responsibilities that follow. Public ownership changes not only the company's financial structure but also its culture, accountability systems, communication requirements, and strategic environment. Successful founders learn how to balance transparency with long-term strategic thinking while maintaining operational discipline under increased public attention.

As alternative public offering structures continue evolving, entrepreneurs who understand these mechanisms gain powerful strategic advantages. Knowledge creates leverage. Founders capable of evaluating multiple pathways can negotiate more effectively, structure transactions more intelligently, and position themselves for stronger long-term wealth outcomes. They are less likely to accept unfavorable terms simply because they believe only one path exists.

The future of public markets will likely continue becoming more flexible, technology-driven, and globally interconnected. Blockchain technology, decentralized finance, tokenized securities, AI-driven financial analysis, retail investor platforms, and digital capital formation tools may continue transforming how businesses access funding and liquidity. Entrepreneurs who understand these trends early may position themselves at the forefront of future financial innovation.

Direct listings represent more than a financial structure. They symbolize a broader movement toward flexibility, transparency, founder empowerment, and market evolution. They reflect a changing world in which businesses increasingly seek alternatives to legacy financial systems that may no longer align perfectly with modern entrepreneurial realities. As capital markets evolve, founders who understand both traditional and non-traditional pathways will possess greater ability to shape their financial futures strategically.

The evolution of modern public offerings is ultimately a story about control, access, innovation, and wealth creation. Companies today no longer operate within a single rigid framework for entering public markets. Instead, they can evaluate multiple strategies, adapt to changing conditions, and structure transactions that better align with their long-term visions. For entrepreneurs, investors, and future business leaders, understanding these alternatives is no longer optional. It is becoming an essential component of modern financial literacy and strategic business planning.

The Founder Who Refused the Traditional IPO

Ethan Morales sat alone in the conference room overlooking downtown Miami long after the rest of his executive team had gone home. The city lights reflected against the glass walls while financial projections covered the massive screen at the front of the room. His company, NexusFlow Technologies, had grown from a two-person startup operating out of a rented apartment into one of the fastest-growing AI workflow platforms in the world. Venture capital firms valued the company at nearly six billion dollars, and Wall Street banks were now competing aggressively to lead its public offering.

Five years earlier, Ethan had nearly gone bankrupt trying to keep the company alive. He maxed out credit cards, sold his condo, and borrowed money from family members while working eighteen-hour days building software nobody initially understood. Most investors rejected him repeatedly. They said the market was too crowded, the technology too ambitious, and the timing too early. But Ethan believed businesses around the world desperately needed AI-driven automation tools capable of replacing repetitive digital workflows.

Now the same financial institutions that ignored him during the early years wanted exclusive access to his company's IPO. Senior bankers flew into Miami weekly carrying glossy pitch books filled with valuation projections, institutional demand estimates, and promises of successful market debuts. They invited Ethan to luxury dinners, private sporting events, and exclusive networking retreats. Every bank promised they could maximize the company's valuation and deliver a successful offering.

At first, Ethan felt excited. Going public had always represented the ultimate milestone in his mind. It meant validation. It meant liquidity for employees who sacrificed years of their lives building the company. It meant global credibility and access to large pools of capital. But as negotiations progressed, something began bothering him.

One evening, Ethan reviewed historical IPO data while preparing for another banker meeting. He noticed a recurring pattern. Numerous companies experienced massive first-day stock price increases immediately after their IPOs. Financial media celebrated these events as triumphs, yet Ethan interpreted the numbers differently. If a company's stock price jumped fifty percent on the first day, it often meant the shares had been sold too cheaply during the offering itself.

The realization disturbed him deeply.

"If our stock jumps fifty percent on day one," Ethan said during a board meeting, "that means we gave away billions of dollars in value."

Some board members dismissed his concerns. They argued that strong first-day performance generated positive headlines and investor confidence. But Ethan could not stop thinking about the implications. He had spent years sacrificing everything to build NexusFlow. Why should institutional investors receive discounted access simply because they had relationships with underwriters? The questions intensified after Ethan met several founders who had recently completed traditional IPOs. Some privately admitted frustration with the process. They described endless roadshows, pricing pressure from underwriters, restrictive lock-up periods, and limited control over share allocations. Several believed their companies had been intentionally underpriced to benefit institutional clients.

One founder leaned across a private dinner table in San Francisco and quietly told Ethan, “The IPO wasn’t designed for us. It was designed for Wall Street.”

That conversation changed everything.

Over the next several months, Ethan began studying alternative public offering structures obsessively. He analyzed direct listings, SPAC mergers, hybrid models, and international listing frameworks. He met with securities attorneys, exchange executives, economists, and founders who pursued non-traditional offerings. The more he learned, the more convinced he became that NexusFlow did not need a traditional IPO.

The company already had millions of users globally. Revenue growth remained explosive. Financial media covered the business constantly. Existing investors wanted liquidity more than the company needed additional capital. NexusFlow possessed strong cash reserves and minimal debt. Ethan began asking a revolutionary question. "What if we go public without a traditional IPO?"

The idea terrified many people around him.

Some board members worried institutional investors would react negatively. Others feared trading volatility without underwriting stabilization mechanisms. Several executives argued Wall Street relationships could become damaged permanently. Traditional investment banks strongly discouraged the idea, warning Ethan that bypassing the conventional IPO process introduced enormous risks.

But Ethan remained unconvinced.

One afternoon, he visited his father in Orlando. His father had worked construction jobs for decades while helping support Ethan's early entrepreneurial ambitions. They sat quietly on the back patio drinking coffee while Ethan explained the situation.

"They want us to follow the system exactly how it's always been done," Ethan said.

His father smiled slightly.

"And do you think you built your company by doing what everybody else did?"

The question stayed with Ethan for weeks.

Eventually, NexusFlow's leadership team voted to pursue a direct listing instead of a traditional IPO. The decision shocked financial media. Analysts debated whether the strategy would succeed or fail. Some praised the company's confidence and innovation. Others warned the market could react unpredictably without traditional underwriting support.

Preparation intensified immediately. Attorneys finalized regulatory filings. Financial teams prepared audited statements. Investor relations executives organized educational presentations for potential shareholders. Exchange officials coordinated listing logistics carefully. Every detail mattered.

Unlike traditional IPOs, NexusFlow would not conduct a massive roadshow designed to market newly issued shares to institutional investors. Instead, the company focused heavily on transparency. Management published detailed financial disclosures, hosted public investor education sessions online, and communicated openly about long-term business strategy.

As listing day approached, volatility spread through financial news networks. Commentators argued constantly about whether direct listings represented the future of public markets or merely a temporary experiment suitable only for elite technology companies.

Ethan ignored most of the noise. On the morning NexusFlow officially became publicly traded, Ethan stood quietly inside the exchange building watching traders, journalists, executives, and employees gather around massive screens. His hands trembled slightly as the opening reference price appeared.

Then trading began.

Within minutes, millions of shares exchanged hands as supply and demand established the company's market value organically. The stock fluctuated aggressively early in the session, but by midday it stabilized well above initial expectations. Financial media exploded with coverage. Analysts debated the long-term implications for Wall Street and future IPO structures.

But for Ethan, the most meaningful moment occurred later that evening.

Several longtime employees gathered at company headquarters after markets closed. Many of them had joined NexusFlow years earlier when salaries were low and success seemed uncertain. Through employee equity ownership, some were now financially independent for the first time in their lives.

One engineer approached Ethan quietly during the celebration.

"My parents worked factory jobs their entire lives," she said. "Today I paid off their mortgage."

Ethan smiled silently.

At that moment, he realized the public listing was never truly about headlines, valuations, or financial prestige. It was about creating opportunity. It was about ownership. It was about empowering the people who believed in the company long before the world recognized its value.

Over the following years, NexusFlow continued growing internationally while maintaining strong founder influence and long-term strategic discipline. Competitors emerged constantly, markets fluctuated, and economic conditions changed, but the company adapted successfully because leadership remained focused on long-term value creation rather than short-term market pressure.

Ethan eventually became known not only as a successful founder, but also as one of the entrepreneurs who helped accelerate the acceptance of alternative public offerings across global markets. Younger founders studied NexusFlow's listing strategy while rethinking how modern companies could approach liquidity, ownership, and public market participation.

Years later, during a university lecture, a student asked Ethan whether he regretted bypassing the traditional IPO process.

Ethan paused thoughtfully before answering.

"The biggest wealth decisions in life usually happen when you stop assuming there's only one path forward."

Chapter 2

Comparing Traditional IPOs vs. Direct Listings

For decades, the traditional initial public offering dominated the financial world as the primary mechanism companies used to transition from private ownership into publicly traded corporations. The process became deeply embedded within global capital markets and was viewed as the gold standard for raising large amounts of capital while establishing institutional credibility. However, as modern financial markets evolved, founders, executives, and investors began exploring alternatives that offered greater flexibility, transparency, efficiency, and control. Direct listings emerged as one of the most important alternatives, fundamentally challenging how businesses think about public offerings and liquidity events.

To understand the significance of direct listings, it is essential to compare them carefully against traditional IPO structures. Although both pathways ultimately allow companies to become publicly traded on major exchanges, the mechanics, incentives, costs, shareholder impacts, pricing methods, and long-term strategic implications differ substantially. These differences can influence everything from founder wealth and ownership dilution to market perception and investor participation.

A traditional IPO typically begins when a private company hires one or more investment banks to act as underwriters. These banks guide the company through the offering process, help prepare regulatory filings, market the company to institutional investors, assist with valuation analysis, and coordinate the public launch. The underwriters effectively serve as intermediaries between the company and the investing public. Their goal is to structure a successful offering that raises capital while creating strong demand for the company's shares.

The process often begins many months before the actual listing date. Companies undergo extensive financial audits, legal reviews, governance restructuring, operational analysis, and regulatory preparation. Investment banks organize investor presentations known as roadshows, where executives meet with institutional investors across major financial centers. During these meetings, company leadership explains its business model, growth strategy, financial performance, competitive advantages, and future opportunities.

As institutional demand develops, underwriters work to determine an offering price. This pricing process is one of the most important and controversial aspects of traditional IPOs. Underwriters attempt to balance investor demand with valuation expectations while ensuring sufficient market enthusiasm once trading begins. Ideally, the stock performs well after listing without becoming excessively volatile. However, critics argue that underwriters often intentionally price IPOs conservatively to benefit institutional clients who receive preferred share allocations.

This issue becomes especially visible when stocks experience dramatic first-day price increases. While headlines often celebrate these "IPO pops," some founders interpret them differently. If shares rise dramatically immediately after trading begins, it may indicate the company sold shares below true market value during the offering itself. In practical terms, the company may have transferred substantial wealth to institutional investors who purchased shares at discounted pre-market prices.

Direct listings attempt to address some of these concerns by restructuring how companies enter public markets. In a direct listing, the company does not rely on a traditional underwriting syndicate to sell newly issued shares in the same manner as a standard IPO. Instead, existing shareholders such as founders, employees, venture capital firms, and early investors can sell their shares directly into the public market once trading begins. Rather than pre-allocating shares to select institutional investors, market supply and demand determine pricing more organically. One of the most important differences between traditional IPOs and direct listings involves capital raising. In a conventional IPO, companies usually issue new shares to raise additional capital for expansion, acquisitions, research, debt reduction, or operational growth. This process increases the company's total share count and may dilute existing shareholders. In contrast, many early direct listings focused primarily on liquidity rather than fundraising. Existing shareholders sold shares directly without the company necessarily issuing large amounts of new stock.

This distinction matters significantly depending on the company's financial condition and strategic objectives. Businesses that urgently need large amounts of capital may still prefer traditional IPOs because underwriters can help guarantee fundraising success. Companies with strong cash reserves and limited immediate capital needs may find direct listings more attractive because they can provide liquidity without substantial dilution.

Another major difference involves underwriting fees. Traditional IPO underwriting fees can be extremely expensive, especially for large offerings. Investment banks often charge percentages of total funds raised, resulting in fees that may reach tens or hundreds of millions of dollars. Direct listings typically reduce these costs substantially because banks play more limited advisory roles rather than fully underwriting the transaction. For founders focused on efficiency and shareholder value preservation, lower transaction costs can become highly attractive.

Lock-up periods also differ between these structures. In many traditional IPOs, insiders and early investors are restricted from selling shares for several months after the offering. These lock-up agreements aim to reduce immediate selling pressure and support stock price stability. However, they can delay liquidity opportunities for employees and early shareholders who may have waited years to monetize their equity. Direct listings often provide greater flexibility by allowing existing shareholders to sell shares earlier without lengthy lock-up restrictions.

Pricing transparency represents another important distinction. Traditional IPO pricing often occurs through private negotiations between underwriters and institutional investors during the roadshow process. Critics argue this system may favor large institutional clients with strong banking relationships. Direct listings allow market-driven supply and demand to play a larger role in determining the opening stock price, potentially improving transparency and pricing efficiency.

However, direct listings also introduce unique challenges and risks. Traditional underwriters often help stabilize stock prices during early trading through various market-support mechanisms. Without these stabilization efforts, direct listings may experience greater volatility, especially during the opening trading sessions. Companies pursuing direct listings must therefore ensure sufficient investor awareness, shareholder participation, and trading liquidity to support healthy market activity.

Brand recognition becomes critically important in direct listings. Companies pursuing this pathway often already possess strong public visibility, extensive customer bases, or significant investor interest before listing. Businesses such as Spotify and Slack succeeded partly because millions of people already understood their products and business models. Lesser-known companies may struggle to generate sufficient investor demand without traditional underwriting promotion and roadshows.

The investor composition may also differ between these offering methods. Traditional IPO allocations frequently favor institutional investors such as hedge funds, pension funds, mutual funds, and large asset managers. Retail investors often gain access only after public trading begins, sometimes at significantly higher prices. Direct listings may create broader access by allowing all investors to participate more equally once trading opens on the exchange. Corporate governance considerations also play important roles in public offering decisions. Founders often worry about maintaining long-term strategic control after becoming public companies. Traditional IPOs may increase institutional investor influence and shareholder activism pressures. Alternative listing structures sometimes provide greater flexibility regarding voting rights, ownership concentration, and governance arrangements.

Public perception also matters significantly. Traditional IPOs still carry strong prestige and credibility within many financial circles. Major investment banks often provide analyst coverage, institutional relationships, and marketing support that can benefit newly public companies. Some investors view direct listings as riskier or less proven structures, although this perception continues evolving as more successful direct listings occur.

The regulatory environment surrounding public offerings continues adapting as financial innovation accelerates. Stock exchanges and securities regulators increasingly support alternative listing structures while attempting to preserve investor protections and market integrity. Regulatory adjustments have gradually expanded the flexibility available for direct listings, including the ability for some companies to raise capital directly through modified listing structures. Another important consideration involves employee equity compensation. Many startups compensate employees heavily with stock options or restricted shares during early growth stages. Liquidity events become critically important because employees may hold substantial paper wealth without immediate access to cash. Direct listings can sometimes create earlier liquidity opportunities compared to traditional IPOs with extended lock-up periods.

Timing flexibility also differs substantially between offering methods. Traditional IPOs require extensive coordination between underwriters, investors, regulators, and exchanges. Market timing becomes extremely important because volatile economic conditions can disrupt offerings unexpectedly. Direct listings may provide somewhat greater flexibility because they depend less heavily on pre-negotiated institutional demand-building processes.

The broader evolution of alternative public offerings reflects deeper changes occurring across global financial markets. Private capital availability has expanded dramatically over the past two decades. Venture capital firms, sovereign wealth funds, private equity groups, family offices, and secondary markets now provide companies with access to enormous private funding pools. As a result, many businesses remain private far longer than previous generations while still achieving multibillion-dollar valuations. This shift changes how companies view public markets. Historically, businesses often pursued IPOs primarily because they needed growth capital unavailable elsewhere. Today, some companies pursue public listings primarily for liquidity, visibility, acquisition currency, or strategic positioning rather than urgent fundraising needs. Direct listings align especially well with businesses that already possess strong financial resources and seek efficient liquidity solutions.

The psychology surrounding founder decision-making has also evolved. Modern entrepreneurs increasingly view public offerings strategically rather than symbolically. They evaluate dilution carefully, analyze transaction costs aggressively, negotiate governance structures intentionally, and think long term about wealth preservation. Founders today possess greater access to financial information, alternative structures, and experienced advisors than previous generations.

Despite growing enthusiasm surrounding direct listings, traditional IPOs remain highly valuable and effective for many businesses. Companies requiring large fundraising rounds, institutional investor support, or market stabilization may benefit significantly from traditional underwriting structures. Some businesses also value the credibility and visibility associated with major Wall Street banking partnerships. The most successful founders recognize that no single structure works universally. Every business possesses unique characteristics that influence which pathway may be most appropriate. Factors such as company size, profitability, industry, brand recognition, capital needs, shareholder composition, market conditions, governance goals, and investor demand all influence the optimal strategy.

Understanding these differences empowers entrepreneurs to make informed decisions rather than blindly following historical norms. Public offerings represent some of the most important financial events in a company's lifecycle. The chosen structure can influence ownership dilution, founder control, employee wealth, investor relationships, media perception, long-term valuation, and strategic flexibility for years or even decades.

As financial markets continue evolving, the distinction between traditional and non-traditional offerings may become increasingly blurred. Hybrid structures, decentralized finance mechanisms, blockchain-based securities systems, auction-based pricing models, and AI-driven capital formation tools may continue reshaping how companies access public markets. Entrepreneurs who understand these evolving frameworks early will likely possess significant strategic advantages in future capital markets. Ultimately, the comparison between traditional IPOs and direct listings is not simply about financial mechanics. It reflects broader questions about fairness, efficiency, transparency, ownership, control, and the future evolution of capitalism itself. As founders gain greater flexibility in how they structure liquidity events, they gain greater power to shape not only their companies' futures but also their personal wealth trajectories and long-term legacies.

Two Founders, Two Paths to Wall Street

Marcus Hill and Daniel Rivera launched their software companies within months of each other. Both founders operated in the rapidly growing artificial intelligence industry, both achieved extraordinary revenue growth, and both attracted significant venture capital investment. Yet despite their similarities, their philosophies about business, ownership, and public markets differed dramatically.

Marcus believed strongly in traditional financial systems. He admired Wall Street institutions, respected investment bankers, and viewed the classic IPO process as a rite of passage for successful entrepreneurs. Daniel, however, approached finance differently. He distrusted unnecessary intermediaries, questioned conventional systems, and constantly searched for more efficient alternatives.

For years, their companies grew side by side as competitors. Marcus built AetherGrid, an enterprise AI infrastructure company specializing in automation for Fortune 500 corporations. Daniel founded LuminaFlow, a creator-focused AI platform helping small businesses automate content, marketing, and customer engagement workflows. Both companies scaled aggressively as artificial intelligence transformed global business operations.

By year six, both businesses surpassed one billion dollars in annual revenue.

Financial media constantly compared the two founders. Business magazines featured them together on conference panels discussing innovation, entrepreneurship, and the future of AI. Venture capital firms competed aggressively to invest additional capital into both companies. Analysts predicted each would eventually become one of the largest public offerings of the decade.

Eventually, Wall Street arrived.

Investment banks flooded both founders with proposals, valuation models, and underwriting presentations. Senior bankers traveled constantly between San Francisco, New York, Miami, and Austin attempting to secure exclusive relationships with the companies. Every major financial institution wanted involvement. Marcus embraced the process immediately. He hired a leading global investment bank and began preparing for a traditional IPO. Massive teams of lawyers, accountants, investor relations consultants, and financial advisors filled AetherGrid's headquarters daily. Roadshow schedules were drafted months in advance. Institutional investor meetings were carefully coordinated. Underwriters organized valuation analyses and pricing discussions constantly.

Marcus enjoyed the prestige surrounding the process.

Private jets transported executives between financial centers. Elite investors attended private dinners and presentations. Financial television networks speculated about AetherGrid's future valuation almost daily. Marcus felt as though he had finally entered the highest levels of global business.

Daniel reacted very differently.

Instead of rushing into underwriting agreements, he spent months researching alternative public offering structures obsessively. He studied direct listings, hybrid offerings, auction-based systems, SPAC mergers, and international exchange models. While Marcus traveled through Wall Street boardrooms, Daniel held long conversations with founders who regretted aspects of traditional IPO structures. One evening, Daniel visited a former tech founder in Los Angeles who recently completed a major IPO. The founder quietly shared frustrations that never appeared in public interviews. "We built the company for twelve years," the founder said. "Then underwriters decided the price behind closed doors. The stock jumped almost seventy percent the first day. Wall Street celebrated, but all I could think about was how much value we gave away."

That conversation changed Daniel's perspective permanently.

Meanwhile, Marcus moved deeper into the IPO process. Underwriters prepared extensive roadshows targeting institutional investors worldwide. Demand appeared extremely strong. Analysts projected enormous enthusiasm once trading began. Marcus trusted the system completely.

But behind the scenes, tension quietly developed.

Several early employees questioned why lock-up agreements would prevent them from selling shares for months after the IPO. Some worried institutional investors would receive preferential allocations while longtime employees remained restricted. Others privately wondered whether underwriters intentionally preferred conservative pricing to benefit large clients.

Marcus dismissed most concerns.

"This is how public markets work," he repeatedly explained.

Daniel disagreed.

After months of analysis, LuminaFlow officially announced plans to pursue a direct listing instead of a traditional IPO. Financial media exploded instantly. Analysts debated whether Daniel was brilliant or reckless. Wall Street executives criticized the decision privately while publicly pretending to remain supportive.

Daniel remained calm.

LuminaFlow already possessed millions of active users globally. Revenue growth remained extraordinary. The company held substantial cash reserves and minimal debt. Daniel believed the company did not require massive fundraising through newly issued shares. Instead, he wanted liquidity opportunities for employees and existing investors without excessive dilution or underwriting control.

The contrast between the two companies became one of the biggest stories in finance.

Marcus prepared for his highly anticipated IPO roadshow while Daniel organized investor education sessions focused on transparency and open market pricing. Financial journalists framed the situation as a battle between traditional finance and modern market innovation.

Then the listings arrived. AetherGrid's IPO launched first.

The opening ceremony looked spectacular. Financial networks broadcast live coverage all morning. Marcus rang the exchange bell surrounded by executives, bankers, and institutional investors. Underwriters celebrated aggressively as demand appeared overwhelming.

But by midday, AetherGrid's stock price surged nearly ninety percent above the IPO offering price.

Television commentators called the launch one of the most successful IPOs in years.

Marcus smiled publicly during interviews, but privately he felt unsettled.

Ninety percent.

The number haunted him.

Late that evening, Marcus sat alone reviewing calculations from the offering. The company had effectively transferred billions of dollars in value during the pricing process. Institutional investors who received pre-market allocations achieved enormous gains almost instantly while employees remained locked out from selling their shares.

For the first time, Marcus began questioning whether the process truly benefited the company as much as Wall Street claimed.

Three months later, LuminaFlow completed its direct listing.

Unlike AetherGrid's massive roadshow-driven launch, LuminaFlow's listing focused heavily on transparency and market-driven pricing. Existing shareholders sold shares directly into the public market while supply and demand established valuation naturally throughout the trading session.

Volatility remained high initially, but trading stabilized successfully by the end of the first day. Financial media quickly acknowledged that the listing worked far better than many critics expected.

Most importantly to Daniel, employees gained immediate liquidity flexibility without restrictive lock-up structures.

Weeks later, Marcus and Daniel met privately at a technology conference in Miami.

Marcus looked exhausted.

Public shareholders pressured AetherGrid aggressively regarding quarterly performance expectations. Analysts criticized minor revenue fluctuations constantly. Employees remained frustrated about lock-up restrictions while institutional investors who received early allocations had already secured massive profits.

Daniel's experience looked different.

LuminaFlow still faced public market pressures, but Daniel retained greater satisfaction regarding how the transition occurred. Employees appreciated the liquidity flexibility. Existing shareholders believed pricing reflected more genuine market demand. Operational focus remained centered more heavily on long-term growth rather than short-term optics.

Over dinner, Marcus finally admitted what had been bothering him for months.

"I think we left too much value on the table."

Daniel nodded quietly.

"The system works well for some people," he replied. "The question is whether it worked best for your company."

Marcus stared silently across the ocean visible beyond the restaurant windows.

For years, he assumed there was only one legitimate path to becoming a public company. Now he realized public offerings were not simply financial transactions. They were strategic decisions shaping ownership, control, employee wealth, long-term flexibility, and founder legacy.

Months later, Marcus began restructuring AetherGrid's future capital market strategy aggressively. He reduced dependence on traditional financing structures, expanded direct shareholder communication, and studied emerging public market innovations much more seriously.

The experience changed him permanently.

Years later, business schools taught both case studies side by side.

One represented the power of traditional Wall Street systems.

The other represented the growing evolution toward founder-driven public market innovation.

And future entrepreneurs studying both stories learned one of the most important lessons in modern finance:

The path a company chooses into public markets can shape not only its valuation, but also its culture, ownership dynamics, long-term flexibility, and the lives of everyone connected to its success.

Chapter 3

The Mechanics of a Direct Listing

Understanding the mechanics of a direct listing is essential for founders, executives, investors, employees, and financial professionals who want to navigate modern public markets strategically. While direct listings may appear simpler than traditional IPOs on the surface, the process still involves extensive preparation, regulatory compliance, financial transparency, investor education, operational coordination, and exchange approval. A successful direct listing requires a company to demonstrate strong organizational maturity, market readiness, and sufficient investor interest before trading begins.

Unlike a traditional IPO, where underwriters actively market and distribute newly issued shares to institutional investors before the stock begins trading publicly, a direct listing allows existing shareholders to sell their shares directly on a public exchange. Instead of relying primarily on investment banks to determine pricing and allocate shares privately, the market itself plays a much larger role in establishing the opening share price through real-time supply and demand dynamics. Although this structure changes several aspects of the public offering process, companies pursuing direct listings must still complete many of the same foundational steps required for traditional public offerings. Public market readiness remains critically important regardless of the listing method selected. Companies must prepare audited financial statements, establish public-company governance systems, implement internal financial controls, satisfy exchange requirements, comply with securities regulations, and prepare management teams for life as a publicly traded organization.

The process usually begins years before the actual listing date. Most successful direct listings involve companies that already possess substantial operational scale, recognizable brands, experienced leadership teams, and significant private investor support. Businesses considering direct listings often spend years building the financial infrastructure necessary to operate under public market scrutiny.

One of the earliest and most important stages involves financial preparation. Public companies must produce accurate, transparent, and highly detailed financial reporting that complies with regulatory standards. Independent accounting firms conduct extensive audits to verify the company's financial statements, revenue recognition methods, liabilities, cash flow reporting, and internal accounting systems. Investors entering public markets demand confidence in the reliability of financial disclosures, and regulatory agencies enforce strict standards surrounding accuracy and transparency.

In addition to financial audits, companies must strengthen corporate governance structures. Public market investors expect clear board oversight, executive accountability, risk management systems, compliance procedures, and transparent reporting frameworks. Many private companies must significantly upgrade these systems before becoming public. Independent directors are often added to boards, governance committees are established, legal compliance systems are expanded, and executive compensation structures are reviewed carefully.

Legal preparation also plays a major role in direct listings. Securities attorneys assist companies in preparing registration documents filed with regulators such as the U.S. Securities and Exchange Commission. These filings contain detailed information about the company's operations, financial condition, leadership, risks, shareholder structure, market opportunities, and business strategy. Transparency becomes one of the most important principles governing public markets.

One of the central documents used in direct listings is the registration statement, often filed using forms similar to those required in traditional IPOs. This filing provides investors with extensive information regarding the company and serves as the foundation for public market disclosure. Regulators review these filings carefully and may request revisions, clarifications, or additional disclosures before approving the listing.

Unlike traditional IPOs, direct listings generally do not involve a conventional underwriting syndicate purchasing shares and reselling them to institutional investors. However, investment banks may still participate as financial advisors. Their role shifts away from underwriting and toward advising the company on market conditions, regulatory compliance, investor education, exchange coordination, and listing execution.

Advisory banks may assist companies in estimating potential investor demand, coordinating shareholder communication, analyzing comparable public company valuations, and preparing executives for public market engagement. However, because they are not underwriting the transaction in the traditional sense, their fees are typically lower than those associated with fully underwritten IPOs.

One of the most unique aspects of a direct listing is the price discovery process. In traditional IPOs, underwriters work closely with institutional investors during roadshows to determine an offering price before trading begins publicly. In contrast, direct listings rely much more heavily on market-driven pricing mechanisms.

Before trading begins, exchanges establish a reference price based on private market transactions, shareholder interest, market conditions, and advisory input. This reference price is not the actual trading price but rather an initial benchmark designed to guide the opening process. Once the market opens, buy and sell orders interact dynamically to establish the real opening trading price based on actual investor demand and shareholder selling activity.

This process can create greater pricing transparency because the market determines value more organically rather than through heavily negotiated institutional allocations. However, it may also introduce higher short-term volatility, particularly during early trading sessions. Without traditional underwriters stabilizing the market, price movements may become more sensitive to order imbalances, investor sentiment, and liquidity conditions.

Liquidity represents one of the most important factors in a successful direct listing. Because no large underwriting syndicate pre-distributes shares systematically, the company must ensure sufficient trading interest exists on both the buy and sell sides of the market. Existing shareholders must be willing to sell enough shares to create healthy trading volume, while investors must be prepared to purchase shares actively once trading begins.

This is one reason why direct listings have historically worked best for highly recognizable companies with strong brand awareness and broad investor interest. Businesses such as Spotify and Coinbase already possessed significant public visibility before listing. Millions of consumers understood their products, financial media covered them extensively, and private market demand remained strong. These conditions helped support liquidity and investor participation during their direct listings.

Another major difference between direct listings and traditional IPOs involves lock-up restrictions. Traditional IPOs commonly impose lock-up agreements preventing insiders and early investors from selling shares for several months after the offering. These restrictions aim to reduce immediate selling pressure and stabilize trading prices. Direct listings often provide more flexibility because existing shareholders may be permitted to sell shares immediately once trading begins.

This flexibility can benefit employees and early investors seeking liquidity after years of holding illiquid private shares.

However, it also creates the potential for larger initial selling pressure if many shareholders decide to sell simultaneously. Managing this balance becomes an important strategic consideration for companies pursuing direct listings.

Investor relations preparation is another critical component of the process. Public companies must communicate effectively with analysts, institutional investors, retail investors, media organizations, regulators, and shareholders. Management teams often undergo extensive training before the listing to prepare for earnings calls, public interviews, investor conferences, regulatory disclosures, and financial reporting obligations.

Unlike traditional IPOs, direct listings may involve less emphasis on formal roadshows and institutional marketing campaigns. However, companies still need strong investor education strategies to help the market understand the business model, financial performance, growth opportunities, and long-term vision. Public market confidence depends heavily on transparency and communication quality.

Technology infrastructure also becomes critically important. Public companies must implement systems capable of handling regulatory reporting, shareholder communication, financial disclosure management, compliance monitoring, cybersecurity protection, and trading coordination. Operational weaknesses that may remain manageable within private companies often become far more dangerous once public market scrutiny intensifies.

Another important factor involves shareholder composition. Direct listings typically involve a mixture of founders, employees, venture capital firms, private equity investors, and other early stakeholders holding shares before the listing. The willingness of these shareholders to sell or retain shares influences trading liquidity, price stability, and market perception significantly.

Companies must also carefully consider market timing. Even strong businesses can struggle during periods of economic uncertainty, rising interest rates, geopolitical instability, or broader stock market volatility. Because direct listings depend heavily on organic investor demand, broader market conditions may significantly influence listing outcomes.

The psychology surrounding direct listings differs from traditional IPOs as well. Traditional IPOs often generate excitement through exclusive institutional allocations, roadshow presentations, and highly choreographed marketing efforts. Direct listings rely more heavily on transparency, open market participation, and investor confidence in the company's fundamentals rather than underwriting-driven momentum. Founders pursuing direct listings frequently emphasize fairness, transparency, efficiency, and market-driven pricing. Many believe direct listings reduce conflicts of interest associated with traditional underwriting structures while allowing broader investor participation. This philosophy aligns especially well with modern technology companies that prioritize decentralization, user empowerment, and innovation.

Regulatory frameworks surrounding direct listings continue evolving as markets adapt to new financial models. Exchanges such as the New York Stock Exchange and NASDAQ have introduced rules supporting greater flexibility in direct listing structures, including the ability for some companies to raise primary capital directly through the listing itself.

This evolution demonstrates how rapidly capital markets continue changing. Financial innovation increasingly challenges historical assumptions regarding fundraising, ownership distribution, liquidity creation, and investor participation. Companies now possess more strategic flexibility than ever before when evaluating public market pathways.

Despite these advantages, direct listings are not appropriate for every business. Companies requiring substantial immediate capital infusions, lacking strong market recognition, or needing extensive institutional support may still benefit more from traditional IPOs. Direct listings require confidence in the company's ability to attract investor interest organically without heavy underwriting support.

The mechanics of a direct listing ultimately reflect a broader shift occurring across modern finance. Public markets are becoming more flexible, transparent, and technology-driven. Founders increasingly seek alternatives that preserve ownership value, reduce unnecessary costs, improve pricing fairness, and align public market transitions more closely with long-term strategic objectives.

Understanding these mechanics provides entrepreneurs with critical knowledge that can shape life-changing financial decisions. Public offerings are not merely administrative transactions. They represent transformational events capable of influencing ownership structures, founder wealth, employee liquidity, investor access, corporate governance, and long-term enterprise growth.

As alternative public offering models continue evolving, entrepreneurs who understand the operational mechanics behind these structures will gain powerful strategic advantages. They will be better prepared to evaluate risks, negotiate terms, structure transactions intelligently, and align public market strategies with long-term wealth creation goals. The future of capital markets may continue moving toward increasingly decentralized, transparent, and flexible systems. Direct listings represent one important step within that broader transformation. For modern founders, understanding how these systems work is becoming an essential part of building and scaling companies in the twenty-first century.

The Day the Market Decided the Price

Sophia Bennett stood quietly inside the trading operations room staring at the giant digital clock counting down the final minutes before her company entered the public markets.

Six years earlier, she built VertexSphere Analytics from a tiny apartment in Tampa after losing her corporate finance job during an economic downturn. What began as a small AI-powered business intelligence platform eventually evolved into one of the fastest-growing enterprise analytics companies in North America. Major corporations relied on VertexSphere software to predict supply chain disruptions, optimize pricing models, and automate financial forecasting.

Now the company was about to become publicly traded through a direct listing.

Around her, lawyers, exchange officials, financial advisors, engineers, and executives moved rapidly between computer terminals monitoring incoming market data. Financial news channels displayed the company logo constantly while analysts debated whether the direct listing would succeed.

Sophia remained calm externally, but internally she felt enormous pressure.

Unlike traditional IPOs, there would be no underwriters controlling the opening price behind closed doors. No institutional investors receiving privileged pre-market allocations. No carefully engineered IPO pop designed by Wall Street banks.

Today, the market itself would decide what VertexSphere was worth.

That reality both excited and terrified her.

Months earlier, Sophia shocked the financial industry by rejecting several major investment banks pushing aggressively for a traditional IPO. The banks promised strong institutional demand, analyst coverage, global roadshows, and valuation support. Some executives within VertexSphere's board strongly preferred the conventional approach.

But Sophia kept returning to one uncomfortable question. "If investors are willing to pay a higher price publicly," she asked repeatedly during meetings, "why should we intentionally sell shares below that value privately first?"

The deeper she studied traditional IPO mechanics, the more skeptical she became. She saw repeated examples of companies leaving enormous amounts of money on the table after heavily underpriced offerings. Founders spent years building companies only to transfer billions in value during the pricing process.

Sophia refused to let that happen if another path existed.

Instead, VertexSphere spent nearly eighteen months preparing meticulously for a direct listing.

The process proved far more complex than most outsiders realized.

Independent auditors reviewed years of financial statements exhaustively. Attorneys prepared massive regulatory filings detailing every aspect of the business. Corporate governance structures expanded significantly. Independent board members joined the company. Cybersecurity systems underwent stress testing. Internal financial controls were redesigned to satisfy public-company standards.

Sophia personally spent hundreds of hours preparing for life as a public CEO.

Media training coaches taught her how to handle aggressive interviews. Investor relations consultants prepared her for quarterly earnings calls. Securities lawyers educated her about disclosure regulations, insider trading restrictions, and shareholder communication rules.

At times, the process felt overwhelming.

One night around 2:00 a.m., Sophia sat alone in the company cafeteria reviewing regulatory documents while exhausted employees worked nearby preparing final exchange submissions.

Her longtime COO, Michael, walked in carrying coffee.

"You know," he said quietly, "most people think direct listings are easier than IPOs."

Sophia laughed tiredly.

"Those people have clearly never prepared for one."

The final weeks before listing became increasingly intense.

Because VertexSphere pursued a direct listing, there was no traditional roadshow where underwriters privately allocated shares to institutional investors. Instead, the company focused heavily on transparency and investor education. Public webinars explained the business model in detail. Financial disclosures were released extensively. Analysts received open access to management presentations. Existing shareholders prepared carefully for potential liquidity opportunities.

Inside the company, emotions varied dramatically.

Some early employees felt excited about immediate liquidity access without restrictive lock-up agreements. Others worried the stock price could become unstable without underwriting support. Venture capital investors debated internally about how many shares to sell initially. Founders who once focused purely on software development suddenly found themselves studying exchange mechanics and trading liquidity.

As listing day approached, media attention intensified.

Financial journalists framed VertexSphere as one of the most important tests yet for modern direct listings. Commentators argued constantly about whether companies truly needed traditional underwriters anymore.

Sophia ignored most of the noise.

The night before the listing, she returned home unusually early. She sat alone on the balcony overlooking downtown Tampa thinking about the journey that led there.

She remembered building the first software prototype on an outdated laptop. She remembered getting rejected by investors repeatedly. She remembered maxing out personal credit cards just to keep payroll alive during difficult months. She remembered convincing talented engineers to accept stock options instead of competitive salaries because the company lacked cash.

Now thousands of employees, investors, and customers depended on what would happen the next morning.

At 9:30 a.m., markets opened.

Buy and sell orders flooded into the exchange system instantly.

Unlike a traditional IPO with a fixed offering price, VertexSphere's opening trade depended entirely on real-time market supply and demand. Exchange officials monitored order imbalances carefully while advisory teams analyzed incoming liquidity data.

Sophia watched silently as tension filled the room.

The stock had not opened yet.

Minutes passed slowly.

Then suddenly, the first trade executed.

The room erupted. Financial news anchors immediately announced VertexSphere's opening price live across global television networks. Within seconds, trading volume exploded as institutional investors, retail traders, hedge funds, pension managers, and existing shareholders entered the market simultaneously.

Volatility surged early.

The stock price moved aggressively during the first hour as the market searched for equilibrium. Analysts debated valuation models constantly on television. Social media exploded with speculation. Trading volume reached extraordinary levels.

Yet something remarkable happened by midday.

The stock stabilized naturally around a valuation significantly above what several investment banks originally proposed during IPO discussions months earlier.

Sophia quietly stared at the trading screens.

The market had spoken.

And the market believed the company was worth more than Wall Street originally suggested.

Late that afternoon, Sophia walked through VertexSphere headquarters while employees celebrated throughout the building. Some cried openly after finally gaining liquidity access to stock they had held for years. Others called family members excitedly. Several younger engineers discussed paying off student loans, buying homes, or helping their parents financially for the first time.

One employee stopped Sophia near the elevator.

“My mother worked three jobs while I was growing up,” he said emotionally. “Today I transferred enough money to retire her.”

Sophia smiled softly.

At that moment, she realized the listing was never simply about valuation metrics or financial headlines.

It was about ownership.

It was about creating opportunities for the people who helped build something meaningful from nothing.

Months later, financial analysts declared VertexSphere’s direct listing one of the most successful modern public offerings outside the traditional IPO structure. Other founders began studying the company's strategy carefully while reconsidering their own future public market plans.

But Sophia viewed the achievement differently.

The most important lesson was not that direct listings were always superior to traditional IPOs. The lesson was that founders now had choices. And in business, few things create more power than understanding you are no longer limited to only one path forward.

Chapter 4

Advantages and Disadvantages of Direct Listings

Direct listings have become one of the most discussed innovations in modern capital markets because they challenge many of the assumptions surrounding traditional IPOs. As more founders, investors, and executives explore alternative methods of taking companies public, understanding the true advantages and disadvantages of direct listings becomes critically important. While direct listings can provide meaningful benefits related to transparency, liquidity, pricing efficiency, and founder control, they also introduce unique risks involving volatility, fundraising limitations, investor support, and market uncertainty.

No public offering structure is universally perfect. Every pathway into public markets involves trade-offs. The most successful founders understand that the goal is not simply to choose the newest or most fashionable option, but rather to select the structure that aligns best with the company's financial condition, shareholder objectives, growth strategy, governance philosophy, and long-term vision. Direct listings can be extremely effective under the right circumstances, but they require careful analysis, operational maturity, and strategic preparation.

One of the greatest advantages of a direct listing is the potential reduction in underwriting costs. Traditional IPOs often involve substantial underwriting fees paid to investment banks coordinating the offering process. These fees are usually calculated as percentages of total funds raised and may amount to tens or even hundreds of millions of dollars for large transactions. Direct listings typically reduce these expenses because investment banks serve more limited advisory roles instead of fully underwriting and distributing the offering.

For founders and shareholders, reducing transaction costs can significantly preserve enterprise value. Every dollar not spent on excessive fees remains within the company or with existing shareholders. This efficiency becomes especially important for highly valuable companies where underwriting fees alone may represent extraordinary sums of money. Many modern founders view these savings as an important advantage, particularly when their businesses already possess strong investor recognition and do not require extensive marketing support.

Another major advantage involves pricing transparency. In traditional IPOs, underwriters work closely with institutional investors during private roadshows to determine the offering price before public trading begins. Critics argue that this system can create conflicts of interest because underwriters may intentionally price offerings conservatively to ensure strong first-day trading performance for institutional clients receiving preferred allocations.

This issue became increasingly controversial as many IPOs experienced massive stock price increases immediately after listing. While media organizations often celebrated dramatic first-day gains, some founders interpreted them differently. If shares surged substantially once trading opened publicly, it often suggested that the company may have sold shares below true market value during the offering itself.

Direct listings attempt to reduce this issue by allowing market supply and demand to determine pricing more organically. Instead of relying heavily on pre-negotiated institutional allocations, investors participate more openly once trading begins. Many founders believe this process creates fairer and more transparent price discovery while reducing the likelihood of excessive underpricing.

Direct listings also provide significant liquidity advantages for existing shareholders. In traditional IPOs, lock-up periods often prevent founders, employees, and early investors from selling shares for several months after the offering. These restrictions aim to stabilize stock prices by reducing immediate selling pressure, but they can delay liquidity opportunities for stakeholders who may have waited years to monetize their equity.

Direct listings frequently provide more flexibility by allowing existing shareholders to sell shares earlier once trading begins. For employees holding stock options or restricted shares, this liquidity can become life-changing. Many startup employees spend years accepting lower salaries in exchange for equity ownership. Earlier liquidity opportunities may allow them to pay off debt, buy homes, support family members, invest, or achieve financial independence.

Another important advantage involves reduced dilution. Traditional IPOs commonly involve issuing large amounts of new shares to raise capital. While fundraising can support company growth, it also increases the total share count and dilutes existing ownership percentages. Direct listings often focus more heavily on enabling liquidity for existing shareholders rather than issuing substantial amounts of new stock.

For founders seeking to preserve ownership and voting influence, reduced dilution can be highly valuable. Ownership percentages matter tremendously over the long term because they influence wealth creation, governance power, strategic control, and future financial flexibility. Many founders view dilution carefully because even seemingly small percentage reductions can represent billions of dollars over time as companies scale.

Direct listings may also improve alignment between founders and retail investors. Traditional IPO allocations often favor institutional investors with strong relationships to underwriting banks. Retail investors frequently gain access only after public trading begins, sometimes at significantly higher prices following strong IPO pops. Direct listings may create broader market access by allowing all investors to participate more equally once trading opens publicly.

This perception of fairness aligns particularly well with many modern technology companies that emphasize openness, decentralization, and community-driven growth. Businesses with strong consumer brands may find that direct listings reinforce their cultural identity by avoiding exclusive institutional allocation systems associated with traditional Wall Street practices.

Another advantage involves strategic flexibility. Companies pursuing direct listings often possess greater control over how they structure their public market transition. Founders may avoid some of the pressure associated with heavily choreographed IPO roadshows and institutional pricing negotiations. This flexibility can allow management teams to focus more heavily on long-term operational execution rather than short-term offering optics.

However, despite these advantages, direct listings also introduce meaningful disadvantages and risks that founders must evaluate carefully.

One of the biggest challenges involves the absence of traditional underwriting stabilization mechanisms. In traditional IPOs, underwriters often help support trading stability during the early days following the offering. They coordinate institutional demand, manage allocations carefully, and may intervene to reduce excessive volatility. Direct listings lack much of this infrastructure, potentially creating greater short-term price fluctuations.

Without strong liquidity and investor participation, stocks entering through direct listings may experience sharp swings during early trading sessions. Volatility can create uncertainty among investors, employees, media organizations, and analysts. Excessive instability may also damage public perception even if the underlying business remains fundamentally strong. Another major disadvantage historically involved limited capital raising. Traditional IPOs allow companies to issue new shares directly to raise large amounts of growth capital. Many early direct listings focused primarily on liquidity for existing shareholders rather than substantial fundraising for the company itself.

Although regulatory developments have expanded flexibility surrounding primary capital raises in some direct listing structures, companies still must evaluate whether they possess sufficient cash reserves and operational resources before choosing this pathway. Businesses requiring immediate large-scale fundraising may benefit more from traditional IPO structures with stronger underwriting support.

Brand recognition also becomes critically important in direct listings. Traditional IPO underwriters help market companies aggressively to institutional investors through roadshows, research coverage, and relationship networks. Lesser-known businesses may struggle to generate sufficient investor awareness without these promotional mechanisms.

As a result, direct listings have historically worked best for companies already possessing strong market visibility, established customer bases, extensive media attention, or significant investor demand before listing publicly. Businesses lacking these advantages may face liquidity challenges or weak investor participation during the public transition process.

Analyst coverage may also develop differently. Traditional underwriters frequently provide research coverage following IPOs, helping institutional investors evaluate the business and increasing market visibility. Direct listings may receive less immediate analyst support depending on how financial institutions view the company and its long-term market potential.

Founders must also recognize that direct listings do not eliminate public market pressures. Once a company becomes publicly traded, management still faces quarterly earnings expectations, regulatory scrutiny, investor activism, media attention, and stock price volatility. Some entrepreneurs mistakenly believe alternative listing structures automatically create more founder-friendly public environments. In reality, public ownership fundamentally changes corporate accountability regardless of the listing method used.

Liquidity flexibility can also create risks. While allowing shareholders to sell shares immediately provides advantages, it may also create large initial selling pressure if many insiders choose to liquidate holdings simultaneously. Investors may interpret aggressive insider selling negatively, potentially impacting market confidence and stock performance.

Another important disadvantage involves uncertainty regarding opening price dynamics. In traditional IPOs, companies know the offering price before trading begins. Direct listings rely more heavily on real-time market supply and demand, creating greater unpredictability surrounding initial valuation. While this process may improve pricing efficiency long term, it can also generate anxiety and volatility during the opening sessions.

The psychological dimension of direct listings should not be underestimated either. Traditional IPOs often create prestige, ceremony, and media excitement associated with the classic Wall Street process. Some executives and investors still view traditional IPOs as symbols of corporate legitimacy and institutional acceptance. Direct listings, although increasingly respected, may still feel unconventional to certain market participants.

The regulatory environment surrounding direct listings also continues evolving. Because these structures remain relatively newer compared to traditional IPOs, rules and market practices may continue changing over time. Companies pursuing alternative structures must work closely with experienced legal and financial advisors capable of navigating evolving regulatory frameworks carefully. Perhaps the most important lesson regarding direct listings is that success depends heavily on alignment between the company's objectives and the offering structure chosen. Direct listings work best under certain conditions. Companies with strong brand recognition, substantial private investor demand, healthy balance sheets, experienced management teams, and limited immediate capital needs may benefit significantly from this approach.

Conversely, businesses requiring extensive fundraising, institutional marketing support, trading stabilization, or broader investor education may benefit more from traditional IPO structures. Neither approach is inherently superior universally. Each serves different strategic purposes depending on the company's circumstances and goals.

Modern founders increasingly understand that public market transitions are not simply financial events. They are strategic decisions capable of influencing ownership dynamics, founder control, employee wealth, investor relationships, governance structures, and long-term enterprise value. Choosing the correct pathway requires careful analysis rather than emotional attachment to any single financial trend.

As global capital markets continue evolving, hybrid models may become increasingly common. Companies may combine elements of direct listings, traditional IPOs, SPAC transactions, private placements, secondary offerings, and decentralized finance systems to create customized public market strategies. Financial innovation continues expanding the range of available options for entrepreneurs worldwide.

Ultimately, the rise of direct listings reflects a broader transformation occurring across modern finance. Founders increasingly demand greater transparency, flexibility, fairness, and efficiency in how companies access public markets. Technology, information access, and private capital expansion have shifted power gradually away from rigid financial gatekeeping systems toward more adaptable market-driven structures.

Entrepreneurs who understand both the advantages and disadvantages of direct listings will possess stronger decision-making capabilities as they scale businesses toward public market opportunities. Knowledge creates leverage. Founders capable of evaluating multiple pathways objectively will be better positioned to protect ownership, maximize long-term wealth creation, and align public market transitions with their broader strategic visions.

The Founder Who Almost Chose the Wrong Path

Elena Ramirez built her cybersecurity company from a small coworking office in Orlando into one of the fastest-growing digital infrastructure firms in the country. Her company, SentinelForge Systems, specialized in AI-powered threat detection for financial institutions, hospitals, and government agencies. After nearly eight years of relentless growth, the company reached a valuation exceeding four billion dollars, and investors began pressuring Elena to take the company public.

At first, the decision seemed simple.

Nearly everyone around her recommended a traditional IPO.

Major investment banks flooded SentinelForge headquarters with presentations promising massive institutional demand, global roadshows, analyst coverage, and strong opening valuations. Private equity investors favored the traditional structure because it felt safer and more familiar. Several board members argued that rejecting a conventional IPO could create unnecessary risks.

Elena initially agreed.

She admired the prestige associated with traditional Wall Street offerings. Financial television coverage, exchange ceremonies, investor conferences, and institutional credibility all appealed to her. After years of sacrifice and pressure, the idea of finally standing on the floor of the New York Stock Exchange sounded exciting.

But something began bothering her during early underwriting discussions.

One afternoon, Elena reviewed a proposed IPO pricing range with her CFO, Marcus Lee. The numbers looked conservative compared to recent private market transactions involving SentinelForge shares.

"Why are we pricing below recent secondary market activity?" Elena asked.

Marcus hesitated before answering carefully.

"The underwriters believe strong first-day performance is important."

Elena stared at the spreadsheet silently.

"So if the stock explodes upward immediately," she asked slowly, "that means we sold it too cheaply?"

Marcus sighed quietly.

"That's one way to look at it."

The conversation unsettled her deeply.

Over the following weeks, Elena studied previous IPOs obsessively. She noticed repeated examples where companies experienced enormous first-day price jumps. Media outlets celebrated these IPO pops as signs of success, but Elena increasingly interpreted them as evidence that companies may have transferred massive value to institutional investors during the pricing process.

The more she researched, the more conflicted she became.

At the same time, several early employees approached her privately regarding lock-up concerns. Many had worked at SentinelForge since the startup years when salaries remained low and survival uncertain. Their stock options represented life-changing wealth, yet traditional IPO structures would prevent them from selling shares for months after the offering.

One engineer explained how his father needed urgent medical treatment overseas. Another employee hoped to buy a home before interest rates increased further. Several quietly admitted they felt frustrated watching institutional investors potentially receive immediate liquidity advantages while employees remained restricted.

Elena listened carefully.

For the first time, she realized the public offering decision affected far more than corporate financing strategy. It would influence the lives of hundreds of people who helped build the company from nothing. One evening, Elena attended a private founder dinner in Miami hosted by several technology entrepreneurs who recently went public. The conversation changed her perspective permanently.

A founder who completed a massive IPO the previous year leaned back in his chair and spoke honestly.

"The bankers called it a successful IPO because the stock doubled on day one," he said. "But all I could think about was how much value we gave away."

Another founder disagreed immediately.

"Yes, but the underwriters stabilized the process. Without them, the stock could've collapsed."

The debate continued late into the night.

Some founders praised traditional IPOs for providing structure, institutional support, and credibility. Others criticized underwriting fees, conservative pricing, and allocation systems favoring large institutional investors.

Elena returned home unable to sleep.

For weeks afterward, she immersed herself in studying alternative public offering structures. She researched direct listings, hybrid offerings, SPAC mergers, auction-based pricing systems, and international exchange models. The more she learned, the more she realized there was no universally perfect solution.

Every path involved trade-offs.

Traditional IPOs provided strong institutional support, analyst coverage, and fundraising capabilities. But they also introduced dilution, underwriting fees, lock-up restrictions, and potential pricing inefficiencies.

Direct listings offered transparency, lower fees, reduced dilution, and earlier shareholder liquidity. But they also involved greater uncertainty, volatility risk, and less underwriting stabilization.

The deeper Elena analyzed the situation, the more she understood that the correct decision depended entirely on SentinelForge's specific circumstances.

Fortunately, the company possessed strong cash reserves. Revenue growth remained extremely healthy. Brand recognition within the cybersecurity industry was substantial. Existing investors primarily wanted liquidity rather than additional fundraising. Operational systems already met public-company standards after years of disciplined financial management.

Gradually, Elena began leaning toward a direct listing.

Not everyone agreed.

Several board members strongly opposed the idea. Some institutional investors worried the market might react unpredictably. Investment banks intensified pressure aggressively, warning about volatility risks and reduced analyst support.

"You're gambling with billions in shareholder value," one banker told her directly.

Elena remained uncertain for weeks.

Then something unexpected happened.

One Saturday morning, she visited the company's Orlando headquarters unexpectedly while reviewing strategic plans. A small group of engineers happened to be working voluntarily on a cybersecurity update for a major hospital client.

Elena sat quietly talking with them for over an hour.

Several employees shared stories about the company's early days. They described sleeping in the office during product launches, working weekends without overtime, and turning down higher-paying corporate jobs because they believed in SentinelForge's mission.

Before leaving, one engineer asked Elena a simple question.

"When we finally go public," he said, "will the people who built this company actually benefit fairly?"

The question stayed in her mind constantly afterward.

Two months later, Elena announced SentinelForge would pursue a direct listing instead of a traditional IPO.

Financial media exploded instantly.

Analysts debated the wisdom of the decision nonstop. Some praised the company's confidence and strong financial position. Others warned the listing could become dangerously volatile without traditional underwriting support.

Inside SentinelForge, reactions varied dramatically.

Employees celebrated the possibility of earlier liquidity access. Some investors remained nervous. Competitors watched carefully. Wall Street executives privately criticized the decision while publicly maintaining diplomatic responses.

The preparation process became intense.

Financial disclosures expanded significantly. Investor education presentations were released publicly. Exchange coordination teams worked constantly. Legal advisors reviewed every document meticulously. Elena spent countless hours preparing for earnings calls, media interviews, and public-company governance responsibilities.

Finally, listing day arrived.

As trading opened, volatility surged immediately. Buy and sell orders flooded into the exchange simultaneously while financial television networks broadcast live coverage nonstop.

The stock fluctuated aggressively during the first hour.

Several board members looked visibly anxious.

Then slowly, something remarkable happened.

The market stabilized naturally at a valuation significantly higher than what underwriters originally proposed during traditional IPO discussions months earlier.

By afternoon, investor confidence strengthened substantially.

Employees throughout the company celebrated emotionally as years of hard work transformed into real financial opportunity.

Some paid off debt immediately. Others helped family members financially. Several longtime employees achieved financial independence for the first time in their lives.

Late that evening, Elena walked alone through the mostly empty headquarters.

She stopped beside a wall displaying photographs from the company's earliest startup days. Tiny offices. Folding tables. Old laptops. Exhausted engineers smiling during impossible deadlines.

At that moment, Elena realized something important.

The goal was never to choose the trendiest public offering structure.

The goal was to choose the structure that aligned best with the company's values, people, financial position, and long-term vision.

Direct listings were not automatically better.

Traditional IPOs were not automatically outdated.

Every path involved advantages and disadvantages.

But founders who understood those trade-offs clearly possessed the power to choose strategically instead of simply following convention.

And that understanding changed everything.

Chapter 5

Pricing, Valuation, and Market Dynamics in Direct Listings

One of the most fascinating and misunderstood aspects of direct listings involves pricing and valuation. Public market valuation is not simply a mathematical formula based entirely on revenue, profit margins, or growth projections. It is a dynamic interaction between financial fundamentals, investor psychology, liquidity conditions, market sentiment, institutional behavior, economic trends, and narrative perception. In direct listings, these forces become even more visible because the market itself plays a larger role in establishing value without the same level of centralized underwriting control associated with traditional IPOs.

To understand why pricing matters so deeply, founders must first recognize that valuation affects far more than headlines or temporary media excitement. Valuation influences ownership dilution, investor confidence, employee wealth, acquisition power, strategic flexibility, market credibility, future fundraising opportunities, executive compensation, and long-term shareholder relationships. The way a company enters public markets and establishes its valuation can shape the business for years or even decades afterward.

Traditional IPOs historically relied heavily on investment banks to coordinate the pricing process. Underwriters organized roadshows, met privately with institutional investors, evaluated demand levels, analyzed comparable public companies, and ultimately helped determine an offering price before shares began trading publicly. While this system created structure and predictability, it also generated significant criticism regarding pricing fairness and conflicts of interest.

Many companies experienced dramatic first-day stock price increases after IPO launches. Media outlets often celebrated these "IPO pops" as signs of successful offerings. However, numerous founders eventually questioned whether these outcomes truly represented success. If shares surged fifty percent or more immediately after trading opened, it often suggested that the offering price may have been set below actual market demand.

This issue became one of the central motivations driving interest in direct listings.

Founders began asking difficult questions. Why should institutional investors receive discounted allocations before public trading begins? Why should underwriters control pricing discussions behind closed doors? Why should companies potentially leave billions of dollars on the table through conservative pricing structures designed partly to reward institutional relationships?

Direct listings attempt to address some of these concerns by allowing supply and demand to play a larger role in determining market value organically. Instead of setting a fixed IPO price distributed through underwriting allocations, direct listings typically establish a reference price used as a starting benchmark before public trading begins. Once markets open, investors and existing shareholders interact directly through buy and sell orders, allowing the market itself to determine the actual trading price dynamically.

This creates an entirely different psychological and financial environment.

In traditional IPOs, pricing largely occurs privately before trading begins. In direct listings, pricing discovery occurs publicly in real time. Investors can watch supply and demand establish valuation livc during the opening sessions. This process often feels more transparent but may also produce greater volatility and uncertainty.

The reference price itself plays an important role in direct listings. Exchanges typically work with financial advisors, market makers, and company representatives to establish an estimated starting point based on private market transactions, investor demand, recent secondary sales, comparable company analysis, financial performance, and broader market conditions.

However, unlike traditional IPO pricing, the reference price does not guarantee where trading will actually begin. Real market demand ultimately determines the opening trade. If buy orders exceed expectations significantly, prices may open much higher. If investor demand appears weaker, prices may open below the reference estimate.

This creates important strategic implications for founders and investors alike.

One major advantage of market-driven pricing is the potential reduction of artificial underpricing. Companies entering through direct listings may capture valuations more closely aligned with real-time investor demand rather than heavily negotiated institutional pricing structures. This can preserve shareholder value and reduce the likelihood of dramatic first-day wealth transfers away from existing owners.

At the same time, market-driven pricing introduces greater uncertainty. Traditional IPOs provide clearer pricing expectations before trading begins. Direct listings expose companies more directly to market sentiment fluctuations, investor psychology, liquidity conditions, and broader economic uncertainty during the opening process.

Liquidity plays a critically important role in these dynamics.

Healthy liquidity allows markets to function efficiently. If sufficient buyers and sellers participate actively, prices tend to stabilize more effectively and reflect broader market consensus. However, weak liquidity can amplify volatility dramatically because relatively small order imbalances may create large price swings.

This is one reason why direct listings historically worked best for highly recognizable companies with strong investor awareness and broad shareholder interest. Businesses such as Spotify and Slack entered public markets with substantial global visibility and large investor audiences already familiar with their products and business models.

Brand familiarity reduces uncertainty, and reduced uncertainty supports healthier pricing behavior.

Valuation itself also depends heavily on comparable company analysis. Investors frequently compare newly public companies against existing public businesses operating within similar industries, growth profiles, or market segments. Revenue multiples, earnings ratios, growth rates, gross margins, customer retention metrics, and operating leverage all influence how investors estimate fair valuation ranges.

However, comparables are never perfect.

Every business possesses unique strengths, risks, leadership quality, scalability potential, competitive positioning, and market opportunities. Investors therefore blend financial analysis with subjective judgment, strategic expectations, and psychological perception when determining value.

Narrative matters tremendously.

Companies perceived as category leaders, disruptive innovators, or long-term platform businesses often receive significantly higher valuations than businesses viewed as commodity providers or temporary trends. Investor belief in future market dominance can dramatically influence valuation multiples even before profitability fully materializes.

This is especially true in technology-driven sectors such as artificial intelligence, fintech, cloud infrastructure, cybersecurity, creator platforms, and software ecosystems. Investors often prioritize future scalability and market leadership potential over short-term earnings because platform businesses may eventually generate enormous long-term economic leverage.

Founder credibility also influences valuation dynamics heavily.

Investors evaluate leadership quality constantly. Founders perceived as visionary, disciplined, transparent, and strategically intelligent often strengthen investor confidence significantly. Conversely, leadership inconsistency, governance concerns, unrealistic projections, or communication problems may weaken valuation support rapidly.

Public markets ultimately price both companies and leadership simultaneously.

Macroeconomic conditions also impact valuation dramatically. Interest rates, inflation expectations, economic growth forecasts, geopolitical instability, market volatility, and investor risk appetite all influence how aggressively investors price public companies.

During periods of low interest rates and strong market optimism, investors may pay extremely high growth multiples for technology companies because future earnings appear more valuable relative to fixed-income alternatives. During periods of rising rates or economic uncertainty, investors often prioritize profitability, cash flow stability, and defensive business characteristics instead.

This means even outstanding companies may experience valuation pressure during difficult market environments unrelated to operational performance itself.

Timing therefore becomes strategically important.

Founders pursuing direct listings must evaluate not only internal readiness but also broader market conditions carefully. Listing during periods of strong investor enthusiasm may support healthier pricing dynamics and stronger liquidity participation. Entering public markets during economic stress or industry pessimism may create unnecessary volatility and valuation pressure.

Another major factor influencing direct listing valuation involves insider selling behavior.

Investors monitor insider activity closely searching for confidence signals. If founders, executives, or early investors aggressively liquidate large portions of holdings immediately after listing, markets may interpret the behavior negatively. Conversely, strong insider ownership retention may strengthen investor confidence regarding long-term growth expectations.

This creates delicate balancing challenges.

Founders and employees often deserve liquidity opportunities after years of sacrifice and illiquid ownership. Yet excessive immediate selling may weaken market psychology. The most successful direct listings frequently involve carefully managed shareholder expectations balancing liquidity access with long-term ownership alignment.

Retail investor participation has also become increasingly important in valuation dynamics.

Digital brokerage platforms, online investing communities, social media sentiment, and retail trading behavior now influence market pricing much more strongly than previous generations. Companies with strong consumer brands or loyal user communities may benefit substantially from retail investor enthusiasm during public listings.

However, retail-driven momentum can also increase volatility.

Emotional trading behavior, speculative excitement, online hype cycles, and rapid sentiment shifts may amplify price fluctuations dramatically. Companies entering public markets must therefore remain disciplined and avoid becoming overly dependent on speculative momentum disconnected from long-term fundamentals.

Market makers and exchange specialists also play important roles in direct listings. These participants help facilitate orderly trading by balancing buy and sell flows while supporting liquidity during opening sessions. Their coordination becomes especially important when volatility intensifies.

Long-term valuation sustainability ultimately depends on execution.

Public markets may initially price companies based heavily on narrative, growth expectations, and investor excitement. Over time, however, operational performance increasingly determines sustainable value creation. Revenue growth, margin expansion, customer retention, innovation capacity, strategic adaptability, and governance discipline all influence whether companies justify or exceed their public valuations.

This is why founders should avoid becoming overly emotionally attached to short-term valuation fluctuations after listing publicly. Market prices may move dramatically in response to sentiment, macroeconomic events, analyst commentary, or temporary news cycles. Sustainable wealth creation depends far more on long-term business execution than daily stock price volatility.

The future of pricing dynamics may evolve even further as financial technology advances.

Artificial intelligence, blockchain settlement systems, decentralized finance infrastructure, tokenized securities, and real-time global liquidity platforms may eventually reshape how markets establish valuations. More transparent, algorithmically assisted, globally connected pricing systems could emerge over time. Yet even as technology changes, human psychology will likely remain central to valuation behavior.

Fear, greed, optimism, uncertainty, confidence, and narrative perception have influenced markets for centuries and will likely continue doing so regardless of technological evolution. Successful founders understand both the mathematical and psychological dimensions of valuation.

Ultimately, pricing in direct listings reflects a broader philosophical shift within modern finance. Markets increasingly seek transparency, fairness, flexibility, and broader participation rather than heavily centralized allocation structures. Direct listings allow companies to rely more heavily on open market forces while challenging traditional assumptions about how public valuations should be established.

Founders who understand these dynamics deeply gain tremendous strategic advantages. They can approach public markets more intelligently, negotiate more effectively, manage investor psychology more carefully, and preserve long-term shareholder value more successfully.

Valuation is never just a number.

It is a reflection of trust, expectation, belief, execution, and the market's collective perception of future possibility.

The Billion-Dollar Pricing Mistake

When NovaCircuit AI prepared for its public debut, everyone expected celebration.

The company had become one of the fastest-growing artificial intelligence chip infrastructure businesses in the world. Its advanced processors powered autonomous systems, AI cloud networks, robotics platforms, and military-grade machine learning applications across dozens of countries.

Private investors valued NovaCircuit at nearly fifteen billion dollars.

Wall Street banks competed fiercely for the offering.

Financial media described founder Ethan Vale as one of the most important technology entrepreneurs of his generation.

Yet inside the company, Ethan felt increasingly uncomfortable.

The deeper he moved into IPO pricing discussions, the more he sensed something fundamentally broken within the process.

Investment bankers repeatedly encouraged conservative pricing.

"We want strong first-day performance," they explained constantly.

At first, Ethan accepted the logic. Strong opening performance sounded positive. Investors would feel confident. Media headlines would celebrate success. Momentum would build quickly.

But one night, while reviewing historical IPO data alone in his office, Ethan noticed a disturbing pattern.

Many companies experienced enormous stock surges immediately after trading began.

Forty percent.

Sixty percent.

Ninety percent.

Some even doubled.

Financial television celebrated these IPO pops enthusiastically.

Ethan interpreted them differently.

"If the stock doubles immediately," he thought, "that means the company sold shares for half of what investors were actually willing to pay."

The realization disturbed him deeply.

The next morning, he confronted the lead underwriter directly during a pricing meeting in Manhattan.

"Explain something to me," Ethan said calmly. "Why is leaving billions of dollars on the table considered success?"

The room became quiet instantly.

The banker smiled carefully before answering.

"Strong first-day performance creates confidence."

"For who?" Ethan asked.

Nobody answered immediately.

That conversation changed everything.

Over the following weeks, Ethan studied direct listings obsessively. He analyzed market structure, liquidity dynamics, investor psychology, pricing mechanics, and alternative public offering models. The more he learned, the more convinced he became that traditional IPO pricing often benefited institutional relationships more than the companies themselves.

Inside NovaCircuit, debate intensified rapidly.

Some board members strongly preferred the traditional IPO. Several venture investors worried a direct listing might become excessively volatile. Bankers warned Ethan repeatedly about the risks of abandoning conventional underwriting structures.

But Ethan could not ignore the numbers.

If NovaCircuit priced conservatively and the stock exploded upward immediately afterward, the company could effectively transfer billions in value during the offering itself.

Eventually, Ethan made the decision.

NovaCircuit would pursue a direct listing instead of a traditional IPO.

Financial media exploded instantly.

Analysts debated whether Ethan was visionary or reckless. Some praised his commitment to market-driven pricing transparency. Others warned the company could face severe volatility without underwriting stabilization support.

Inside NovaCircuit headquarters, employees reacted emotionally.

Many supported the decision because they wanted broader liquidity flexibility and fairer market participation. Others worried uncertainty might hurt the stock.

Ethan understood both perspectives.

“The market should decide the value,” he told employees during an internal meeting. “Not a private negotiation behind closed doors.”

Preparation intensified over the following months.

Financial disclosures expanded dramatically. Investor education campaigns launched globally. Exchange officials coordinated opening procedures carefully. Existing shareholders prepared for liquidity opportunities while analysts attempted to estimate where the market might ultimately price the company.

As listing day approached, tension became overwhelming.

The night before trading began, Ethan barely slept.

At sunrise, he stood alone inside NovaCircuit headquarters overlooking Miami's skyline while financial news networks speculated constantly about the upcoming opening price.

He understood the risks.

If investor demand weakened unexpectedly, the stock could collapse publicly. Media criticism would become brutal. Competitors would attack aggressively. Investors might lose confidence.

But Ethan also believed something more important was at stake.

Fairness.

Transparency.

Market-driven value discovery.

At 9:30 a.m., trading officially opened.

But NovaCircuit shares did not begin trading immediately.

Buy and sell orders flooded the exchange system at extraordinary speed while officials attempted to establish equilibrium between demand and supply. Financial television anchors narrated every moment dramatically.

Minutes passed slowly.

Then the opening trade finally executed.

The stock opened significantly above the valuation range originally proposed by traditional underwriters months earlier.

Inside NovaCircuit headquarters, employees erupted emotionally.

But the real shock came afterward. As trading continued throughout the day, investor demand remained extremely strong. The stock fluctuated aggressively early but gradually stabilized at levels far exceeding what Ethan believed the company would have received through the original IPO pricing structure.

By market close, analysts estimated the company avoided leaving nearly four billion dollars in value on the table compared to the original IPO proposal.

Four billion.

The number spread through financial media instantly.

Wall Street executives privately criticized the outcome while publicly congratulating the company diplomatically. Younger founders across Silicon Valley began studying NovaCircuit's listing strategy intensely.

Late that evening, Ethan walked quietly through the mostly empty engineering floors inside headquarters.

Many employees still remained there celebrating.

One engineer approached him emotionally.

"My family immigrated here with nothing," she said. "Today my parents became financially secure because of this company."

Ethan smiled softly. At that moment, he realized the listing was never simply about stock pricing.

It was about ownership.

It was about preserving the value created by the people who spent years building something extraordinary.

Months later, business schools began teaching the NovaCircuit direct listing as one of the most important valuation case studies in modern capital markets.

Students debated whether the company proved traditional IPO systems consistently undervalued innovative businesses.

Investors debated whether direct listings represented the future of market-driven pricing.

But Ethan viewed the lesson more simply.

"The market should decide what a company is worth," he later explained during an interview. "Not a negotiation designed primarily to protect old financial systems."

And after NovaCircuit's success, many founders started asking themselves the same question Ethan asked months earlier inside that Manhattan conference room:

If investors are truly willing to pay more, why should companies intentionally sell themselves for less?

Chapter 6

Investor Psychology and Market Perception in Direct Listings

One of the most overlooked yet critically important aspects of direct listings involves investor psychology and market perception. Financial markets are driven not only by numbers, revenue growth, valuation models, and financial statements, but also by emotion, confidence, narrative, trust, fear, momentum, and perception. Public offerings are psychological events as much as they are financial transactions. The success or failure of a direct listing often depends heavily on how investors interpret the company's strategy, leadership, credibility, timing, and long-term potential.

Traditional IPOs evolved over decades partly because they created structured systems designed to manage investor psychology carefully. Investment banks coordinated roadshows, built institutional demand, generated media excitement, and engineered highly choreographed market debuts. Underwriters often acted as confidence builders, helping reassure institutional investors that the company had undergone extensive vetting and possessed strong support from sophisticated financial institutions. Direct listings fundamentally alter many of these psychological dynamics.

Instead of relying heavily on underwriters to shape investor perception, companies entering through direct listings must build confidence more organically. Investors must evaluate the company's fundamentals, leadership quality, transparency, financial strength, and market position with fewer traditional institutional signals guiding their decisions. As a result, investor psychology becomes even more important.

One of the first psychological questions investors ask regarding any direct listing is simple: "Why did the company choose this path?" The answer to this question can influence perception dramatically. If investors believe a company pursued a direct listing because it possesses strong brand recognition, substantial liquidity, healthy financials, and confidence in its long-term prospects, the decision may be viewed positively. However, if investors suspect the company avoided a traditional IPO because of weak institutional demand, financial instability, or fundraising challenges, perception may quickly turn negative.

This demonstrates an important reality about public markets: perception shapes valuation. Two companies with nearly identical financial performance may receive vastly different market reactions depending on investor confidence, media narratives, leadership reputation, and psychological momentum. Markets are not perfectly rational systems. They are emotional ecosystems influenced by stories, expectations, and collective behavior.

Founders pursuing direct listings must therefore understand narrative control carefully. Modern public markets reward companies capable of communicating compelling long-term visions while maintaining transparency and credibility. Investors want to understand not only what a company does, but also why it matters, how it scales, what competitive advantages protect it, and whether management possesses the discipline required to navigate public market pressures successfully.

Companies such as Spotify and Coinbase succeeded partly because investors already understood their businesses before the listings occurred. Millions of consumers interacted with their products directly. Financial media covered them extensively. Strong brand familiarity reduced uncertainty and strengthened investor confidence.

Familiarity plays a major role in investor psychology. Investors naturally feel more comfortable allocating capital toward businesses they recognize and understand. Companies with strong public visibility often benefit from reduced psychological barriers because investors already possess some degree of trust and awareness. This is one reason why direct listings historically worked best for recognizable technology brands with large user communities and substantial media presence.

Trust is another foundational psychological factor in public markets. Investors constantly evaluate whether management teams appear competent, transparent, disciplined, and aligned with shareholder interests. Direct listings can sometimes strengthen trust because they signal that management believes market-driven price discovery is preferable to heavily controlled institutional allocation systems.

Many investors view this transparency positively. They appreciate structures that reduce potential conflicts of interest associated with traditional underwriting processes. Some retail investors especially favor direct listings because they perceive them as fairer and more accessible compared to IPO systems where institutional investors often receive preferred treatment.

However, investor psychology can also create disadvantages for direct listings. Some market participants still view traditional IPOs as safer, more established, and more credible because underwriters provide perceived validation. Large investment banks serve not only financial functions but also psychological functions. Their involvement signals institutional confidence to many investors. Without strong underwriting support, some investors may perceive direct listings as riskier or less stable, even if the underlying company remains fundamentally strong. This perception may influence trading behavior, analyst coverage, institutional participation, and media narratives during the early phases of public trading.

Volatility itself also influences investor psychology powerfully. Traditional IPOs often benefit from stabilization mechanisms and carefully managed allocations that reduce extreme price swings immediately after listing. Direct listings may experience sharper volatility because prices depend more heavily on real-time supply and demand dynamics.

When investors observe rapid price fluctuations, emotional reactions often intensify. Fear, greed, uncertainty, and momentum-driven trading behaviors can become amplified. Some investors may panic during early volatility while others become excessively speculative. Media organizations often magnify these reactions further by framing volatility dramatically in headlines and financial commentary.

This creates an important challenge for companies pursuing direct listings. Management teams must prepare investors psychologically for the possibility of early volatility while reinforcing long-term strategic confidence. Founders who communicate clearly and maintain emotional discipline during market turbulence often strengthen investor trust over time.

Leadership psychology becomes especially important in this environment. Public market investors evaluate founders constantly. Every interview, earnings call, shareholder letter, and public statement influences market perception. Investors study body language, tone, confidence, consistency, and emotional reactions carefully.

Founders who appear calm, transparent, and strategically focused during volatile periods often inspire confidence. Conversely, executives who appear defensive, emotional, inconsistent, or reactive may unintentionally increase investor anxiety. Public markets reward leadership stability because investors associate emotional discipline with operational discipline.

Another major psychological factor involves liquidity expectations. Investors entering direct listings often pay close attention to insider selling behavior. If founders, executives, or early investors sell large portions of their holdings immediately, markets may interpret the activity negatively. Investors may wonder whether insiders lack confidence in long-term growth prospects.

At the same time, reasonable insider liquidity is natural and expected. Many founders and employees spend years building companies without meaningful liquidity opportunities. Investors generally understand that some selling activity will occur after public listings. The psychological challenge involves balancing liquidity access with long-term confidence signaling.

Employee psychology also matters significantly. Public listings transform internal company culture. Employees who once focused exclusively on product development and operational growth suddenly become aware of stock prices, market commentary, analyst opinions, and financial headlines. Emotional reactions inside the company can shift dramatically during periods of market volatility.

Strong leadership becomes essential during this transition. Founders must help employees maintain long-term focus rather than becoming emotionally consumed by daily stock price movements. Companies that build cultures emphasizing mission, execution, and sustainable growth often navigate public market transitions more successfully than organizations driven primarily by short-term valuation excitement.

Media perception further amplifies investor psychology. Financial media outlets constantly search for compelling narratives surrounding public companies. A direct listing may be framed as visionary innovation or dangerous experimentation depending on how journalists interpret the story. Positive media narratives can strengthen investor enthusiasm while negative narratives may increase skepticism and volatility.

This is why communication strategy matters tremendously before and after direct listings. Successful companies proactively educate investors, analysts, journalists, and shareholders about why the chosen structure aligns with the company's goals and long-term vision. Clear communication reduces uncertainty, and reduced uncertainty often strengthens investor confidence.

Social psychology also plays a major role in modern markets. Investors are heavily influenced by crowd behavior, online discussions, analyst opinions, social media sentiment, and institutional participation trends. Momentum investing has become increasingly powerful within modern financial ecosystems driven by digital communication platforms.

As a result, perception can become self-reinforcing. Positive investor sentiment attracts additional buyers, increasing momentum and strengthening market confidence. Negative sentiment may trigger selling pressure, media criticism, and further uncertainty. Understanding these feedback loops is essential for founders navigating public markets.

Institutional investor psychology differs somewhat from retail investor psychology as well. Institutional investors often focus heavily on liquidity, governance quality, financial predictability, analyst coverage, and long-term strategic positioning. Retail investors may be influenced more strongly by brand recognition, founder personality, media narratives, product familiarity, and social sentiment.

Successful direct listings often appeal effectively to both groups. They combine strong operational fundamentals with compelling narratives, transparent leadership, recognizable brands, and credible long-term growth opportunities.

Another important psychological dynamic involves scarcity and exclusivity. Traditional IPOs often generate excitement partly because institutional allocations are limited and difficult to access. This scarcity can increase perceived value and speculative enthusiasm. Direct listings reduce some of this exclusivity because trading access becomes more broadly available immediately once the market opens.

Some critics argue this may reduce hype-driven demand. Others believe it creates healthier and more sustainable market participation. Both perspectives contain elements of truth. The key lesson is that market structure influences psychology, and psychology influences valuation behavior.

Long-term investor perception ultimately depends on execution. While listing structure matters initially, sustained public market success depends far more on operational performance over time. Companies that consistently grow revenue, maintain strategic discipline, communicate transparently, and execute effectively eventually build strong market credibility regardless of how they entered public markets.

Founders sometimes overestimate the long-term importance of the listing event itself while underestimating the importance of post-listing execution. The public offering may attract enormous attention temporarily, but markets eventually focus primarily on fundamentals. Sustainable value creation requires operational excellence long after the opening bell ceremony ends.

As financial markets continue evolving, investor psychology surrounding direct listings may continue changing as well. Younger investors often view alternative structures more favorably than previous generations because they value transparency, decentralization, fairness, and technology-driven innovation. Institutional acceptance of direct listings may continue strengthening as more successful examples emerge.

The future of public markets will likely involve increasing experimentation with new structures, hybrid models, decentralized systems, and technology-driven capital formation mechanisms. Investor psychology will continue adapting alongside these innovations. Founders who understand how markets think emotionally, not just financially, will possess enormous strategic advantages.

Ultimately, direct listings reveal an important truth about capital markets: valuation is influenced not only by financial performance, but also by trust, narrative, perception, confidence, leadership, and collective psychology. Founders who understand these dynamics deeply can shape investor behavior more effectively while building stronger long-term relationships with public shareholders.

Public markets are human systems. And human systems are driven by psychology as much as mathematics.

The Stock Everyone Was Afraid to Buy

When OrionLink Technologies announced plans for a direct listing, the financial world reacted with immediate skepticism.

The company operated one of the fastest-growing artificial

intelligence logistics platforms in the world, helping manufacturers predict supply chain disruptions before they occurred. Revenue had exploded over the previous four years. Major global corporations depended on OrionLink software to manage inventory forecasting, shipping optimization, and AI-driven purchasing decisions.

On paper, the business looked extraordinary.

Yet investors remained nervous.

The company's founder and CEO, Nathan Cole, understood why.

Three years earlier, a highly publicized technology direct listing collapsed after severe volatility destroyed investor confidence during the first weeks of trading. Financial media repeatedly referenced that failure while discussing OrionLink's upcoming market debut. Analysts questioned whether the company should pursue a safer traditional IPO instead.

Nathan listened carefully to the criticism.

Privately, some board members worried the market simply was not psychologically prepared for another major direct listing after recent failures. Several institutional investors advised OrionLink to hire underwriters and avoid unnecessary risk.

But Nathan believed the market misunderstood the situation entirely.

The problem with the failed direct listing years earlier was not the structure itself. The problem was investor trust. That company entered public markets with weak communication, inconsistent financial disclosures, and unrealistic growth projections. When volatility appeared, investors panicked because confidence in leadership was already fragile.

Nathan refused to repeat those mistakes.

Months before the listing, OrionLink launched one of the most transparent investor education campaigns Wall Street had ever seen. Instead of hiding behind vague corporate language, the company openly explained every aspect of its business model, revenue streams, operational risks, AI infrastructure costs, customer retention metrics, and long-term growth strategy.

Executives hosted live public webinars answering difficult investor questions directly. Engineers demonstrated the software publicly. Customers shared real-world case studies showing how OrionLink prevented millions of dollars in supply chain losses during global disruptions.

Nathan personally appeared in dozens of interviews explaining why the company chose a direct listing.

"We want market-driven pricing," he repeated constantly. "We want transparency. We want equal access. We want investors evaluating the company based on fundamentals, not artificial scarcity."

Some investors appreciated the openness immediately.

Others remained deeply skeptical.

Financial television commentators questioned whether Nathan sounded overly idealistic. Several hedge fund managers privately warned clients to avoid the stock during early trading because volatility risk appeared high.

Inside OrionLink headquarters, employees followed the media coverage nervously.

One afternoon, a young engineer named Kevin approached Nathan after an internal meeting.

"Do you think people are afraid of the company?" Kevin asked quietly.

Nathan smiled thoughtfully.

"No," he replied. "I think people are afraid of uncertainty."

That distinction became the foundation of OrionLink's entire market strategy.

Nathan understood that investor psychology depended heavily on reducing uncertainty. The more transparent the company became, the more confidence investors would eventually develop. He believed trust could overcome fear if communication remained disciplined and consistent. Still, pressure intensified as listing day approached.

Several major investment banks criticized the direct listing publicly. Analysts debated whether OrionLink's valuation remained sustainable. Online forums exploded with speculation. Some retail traders became wildly optimistic while others predicted disaster.

The emotional atmosphere surrounding the listing became increasingly unstable.

The night before trading began, Nathan walked alone through the nearly empty headquarters building. Computer screens glowed quietly across engineering floors where teams had worked for years building the company's AI systems.

He remembered the early days vividly.

Back then, nobody believed predictive logistics AI could scale globally. Investors rejected the idea repeatedly. Nathan survived by sleeping in cheap apartments, coding through the night, and convincing exhausted engineers to keep believing when funding nearly disappeared.

Now billions of dollars depended on how the market perceived the company.

At 9:30 a.m. the next morning, trading officially opened.

But OrionLink shares did not begin trading immediately.

Buy and sell orders flooded into the exchange at extraordinary speed while officials attempted to establish an opening price. Financial news channels broadcast live speculation nonstop. Social media exploded with emotional reactions ranging from extreme excitement to complete panic.

Inside OrionLink headquarters, tension became unbearable.

Employees crowded around giant monitors watching exchange updates refresh constantly.

Still no opening trade.

Minutes passed.

Then suddenly, the first transaction executed.

The stock opened sharply higher than private market estimates.

Within seconds, volatility intensified dramatically.

The price surged upward, then dropped aggressively, then surged again as competing waves of optimism and fear collided in real time. Financial television anchors described the trading session as chaotic. Analysts debated whether the volatility represented healthy price discovery or dangerous instability.

Nathan remained calm publicly despite enormous internal pressure. Throughout the day, he refused to comment emotionally about short-term price movements. During interviews, he repeated the same disciplined message.

"We built the company for long-term value creation. Markets take time to establish fair pricing."

By afternoon, something unexpected began happening.

The volatility gradually slowed.

Institutional investors who initially avoided the stock started analyzing OrionLink's financial disclosures more seriously. Customers publicly praised the company online. Employees remained confident internally. Analysts acknowledged the transparency of management communication.

Trust began replacing uncertainty.

By the end of the first week, the stock stabilized significantly above initial expectations.

More importantly, investor perception changed completely.

Financial media shifted from questioning whether the direct listing would fail to discussing whether OrionLink had established a new model for investor communication and transparency. Several institutional funds increased positions aggressively after concluding management credibility appeared unusually strong.

Months later, during an investor conference in New York, a hedge fund manager approached Nathan privately.

"I avoided your stock initially," the investor admitted. "The market psychology around direct listings still scared people."

Nathan nodded.

"I understand."

"But your transparency changed that," the investor continued. "People eventually trusted the company."

Nathan smiled slightly.

That was the real lesson.

Markets are not driven purely by spreadsheets and valuation formulas.

They are driven by confidence.

And confidence is built through trust, transparency, consistency, and leadership discipline during moments of uncertainty.

Years later, OrionLink became one of the most respected public technology companies in the logistics industry. Business schools studied the company's direct listing strategy extensively, especially its communication approach during volatile market conditions.

But inside OrionLink headquarters, employees remembered a simpler lesson from those stressful early trading days:

Investors are not always afraid of risk.

Most of the time, they are simply afraid of uncertainty.

And the companies that learn how to reduce uncertainty often gain enormous advantages in public markets.

Nathan smiled slightly.

That was the real lesson.

Markets are not driven purely by spreadsheets and valuation formulas.

They are driven by confidence.

And confidence is built through trust, transparency, consistency, and leadership discipline during moments of uncertainty.

Years later, OrionLink became one of the most respected public technology companies in the logistics industry. Business schools studied the company's direct listing strategy extensively, especially its communication approach during volatile market conditions.

But inside OrionLink headquarters, employees remembered a simpler lesson from those stressful early trading days.

Investors are not always afraid of risk.

Most of the time, they are simply afraid of uncertainty.

And the companies that learn how to reduce uncertainty often gain enormous advantages in public markets.

Chapter 7

Regulatory Requirements and Exchange Rules for Direct Listings

Direct listings may represent an innovative alternative to traditional IPOs, but they still operate within one of the most heavily regulated financial environments in the world. Public markets function on trust, transparency, disclosure, and investor protection. Without clear rules and regulatory oversight, capital markets would quickly become unstable, manipulative, and dangerous for investors. As a result, companies pursuing direct listings must comply with extensive legal, financial, governance, reporting, and exchange requirements before their shares can trade publicly.

Many founders initially assume that direct listings involve fewer regulatory obligations than traditional IPOs because they avoid certain underwriting structures. In reality, the regulatory burden remains substantial. Although the mechanics of share distribution differ, companies entering public markets through direct listings still become fully regulated public companies subject to ongoing disclosure obligations, financial reporting standards, governance requirements, insider trading rules, and exchange compliance obligations. Understanding these regulatory frameworks is essential because failure to comply can create devastating consequences. Regulatory violations may lead to delayed listings, financial penalties, shareholder lawsuits, reputational damage, exchange delisting, executive liability, or even criminal investigations in severe cases. Public markets reward transparency and punish companies that fail to meet disclosure expectations.

The foundation of public market regulation in the United States centers heavily around the U.S. Securities and Exchange Commission, commonly known as the SEC. The SEC oversees securities markets, enforces disclosure requirements, investigates fraud, and establishes rules designed to protect investors while maintaining fair and orderly markets.

Before a company can complete a direct listing, it must file detailed registration documents with the SEC. These filings provide investors with extensive information regarding the company's financial condition, business operations, leadership team, governance structure, market risks, legal exposures, revenue sources, growth strategy, shareholder ownership, and competitive landscape.

One of the most important documents within this process is the registration statement. This filing contains audited financial statements, management discussion and analysis sections, risk factor disclosures, executive compensation information, legal proceedings, and detailed operational explanations. Investors rely heavily on these disclosures when evaluating whether to purchase shares in newly public companies.

The SEC reviews these filings carefully and frequently issues comments requiring revisions, clarifications, or additional disclosures before approving the registration process. This review period can become lengthy and highly detailed, especially for complex businesses operating in rapidly evolving industries such as artificial intelligence, biotechnology, cryptocurrency, fintech, or cybersecurity.

Transparency represents the core principle underlying these regulations. Public investors must receive accurate and material information necessary to make informed investment decisions. Companies cannot selectively disclose critical financial or operational information to certain investors while withholding it from the broader market. Fair disclosure rules aim to ensure equal access to important information.

Direct listings still require audited financial statements prepared according to strict accounting standards. Independent accounting firms examine the company's revenue recognition practices, liabilities, internal controls, expense reporting, cash flow management, debt obligations, and overall financial reporting systems. Auditors must certify that the company's financial statements accurately reflect its financial condition.

This process often becomes one of the most difficult transitions for rapidly growing private companies. Many startups initially operate with less formal accounting systems suitable for private operations but insufficient for public market scrutiny. Before listing publicly, companies must strengthen internal financial controls significantly.

The importance of internal controls increased dramatically after major corporate scandals involving companies such as Enron and WorldCom revealed severe accounting fraud and governance failures. In response, lawmakers passed the Sarbanes-Oxley Act, commonly called SOX, which introduced strict corporate governance and financial reporting requirements for public companies.

Under these regulations, management teams must certify the accuracy of financial statements personally. Companies must establish internal systems capable of preventing fraud, detecting accounting irregularities, and ensuring reliable reporting processes. Independent auditors also review the effectiveness of these internal control systems.

Corporate governance requirements represent another major component of public market regulation. Exchanges such as the New York Stock Exchange and NASDAQ impose listing standards related to board composition, audit committees, shareholder voting rights, governance independence, and executive accountability.

Most public companies must maintain independent directors on their boards to help oversee management objectively. Audit committees responsible for financial oversight must typically consist primarily of independent directors with financial expertise. Compensation committees reviewing executive pay structures often require similar independence standards.

These governance systems aim to reduce conflicts of interest while protecting shareholders from excessive managerial control or misconduct. Public companies operate under significantly higher accountability standards than private businesses because millions of investors may depend on the integrity of management decisions and disclosures.

Exchange listing requirements also include minimum financial and operational standards. Companies generally must satisfy thresholds involving market capitalization, shareholder equity, trading volume expectations, public float requirements, and shareholder distribution levels before exchanges approve listings.

Public float refers to the portion of shares available for public trading rather than closely held insider ownership. Exchanges require sufficient public float to support healthy trading liquidity and orderly market functioning. Companies with excessively concentrated ownership structures may struggle to satisfy listing requirements.

Another important regulatory issue involves insider trading rules. Once companies become public, executives, employees, directors, and large shareholders face strict limitations regarding securities transactions based on nonpublic material information. Insider trading violations represent some of the most aggressively prosecuted financial crimes within capital markets.

Public companies must establish compliance systems designed to prevent improper trading activity. Trading windows, blackout periods, disclosure protocols, and legal oversight become essential operational functions after listing publicly. Executives often require extensive training regarding securities law obligations and transaction restrictions.

Disclosure obligations continue long after the direct listing itself. Public companies must file ongoing quarterly and annual reports with regulators, including updated financial statements, operational developments, risk disclosures, executive compensation information, and material business changes. Quarterly earnings reports become especially important because investors and analysts monitor them closely to evaluate performance trends, growth expectations, profitability metrics, and strategic execution. Companies failing to meet disclosure deadlines or reporting standards may face regulatory penalties or exchange sanctions.

Material event disclosure requirements also create significant obligations. Public companies must disclose important developments capable of influencing investor decisions. Examples include mergers, acquisitions, leadership changes, cybersecurity breaches, litigation developments, bankruptcy risks, major customer losses, financing transactions, or regulatory investigations.

Direct listings may also involve unique regulatory considerations regarding shareholder sales and liquidity. Because existing shareholders often sell shares directly into public markets without traditional lock-up restrictions, regulators and exchanges pay close attention to market integrity, disclosure timing, and trading fairness during the opening process.

Exchange coordination becomes highly important during direct listings because pricing depends heavily on real-time supply and demand dynamics rather than fixed offering prices established beforehand. Exchanges monitor order flows carefully to help establish orderly opening trades while reducing extreme market disruptions.

The regulatory environment surrounding direct listings continues evolving because these structures remain relatively newer compared to traditional IPOs. Exchanges and regulators have gradually modified rules to support alternative public offering structures while maintaining investor protections.

For example, regulators eventually approved frameworks allowing certain direct listings to raise primary capital directly rather than focusing solely on secondary shareholder sales. These changes expanded flexibility for companies seeking both liquidity and fundraising opportunities through alternative listing pathways.

International regulations add further complexity for global businesses. Companies operating across multiple jurisdictions may face overlapping disclosure standards, accounting frameworks, securities regulations, tax obligations, and governance expectations. Cross-border listings require sophisticated legal coordination and compliance infrastructure.

Technology companies face additional scrutiny in certain areas involving cybersecurity, data privacy, artificial intelligence ethics, consumer protection, and intellectual property risks. Regulators increasingly examine whether public companies adequately disclose technology-related risks capable of impacting operations or investor value.

Environmental, social, and governance considerations, commonly called ESG factors, also influence modern regulatory environments increasingly. Investors and regulators now expect greater transparency regarding sustainability practices, diversity initiatives, climate-related risks, labor conditions, and governance policies.

The rise of retail investing has further intensified regulatory attention surrounding transparency and market fairness. Digital trading platforms, social media-driven speculation, meme stock volatility, and decentralized financial communities have changed how regulators view market behavior and investor protection responsibilities.

For founders, adapting to this highly regulated environment often requires major psychological and operational adjustments. Private companies frequently operate with greater confidentiality and flexibility. Public companies must embrace transparency as a core operational principle.

This transition can feel uncomfortable initially. Executives accustomed to controlling information tightly may struggle with disclosure obligations requiring broad public communication. However, transparency ultimately strengthens market trust and long-term investor confidence when managed properly.

Strong compliance cultures become essential for long-term success. Companies treating regulation merely as a legal burden often struggle publicly. In contrast, organizations embracing governance discipline, financial transparency, ethical leadership, and shareholder accountability frequently build stronger investor relationships and more sustainable market reputations over time.

Regulatory preparation should begin years before any planned direct listing. Companies that delay governance improvements, financial control upgrades, or compliance infrastructure development often encounter costly delays and operational stress during the listing process.

Experienced legal advisors, auditors, investment bankers, governance consultants, and compliance professionals play critical roles throughout this preparation. Public market transitions involve enormous complexity, and founders rarely navigate them successfully without sophisticated professional guidance.

Despite the regulatory burden, public markets continue offering extraordinary wealth creation opportunities for businesses capable of meeting these standards successfully. Regulations exist not simply to create bureaucracy, but to support trust within financial systems. Trust allows investors to allocate capital confidently, and capital allocation drives economic growth, innovation, and entrepreneurship globally.

Direct listings demonstrate that financial innovation can evolve within regulatory frameworks rather than outside them. Alternative public offering structures still depend fundamentally on transparency, investor confidence, governance integrity, and market fairness. Founders who understand these principles deeply position themselves far more effectively for long-term public market success.

Ultimately, regulation and innovation are not enemies. Healthy financial systems require both. Innovation expands opportunity, while regulation preserves trust. The future of public markets will likely continue balancing these forces as technology, globalization, and investor behavior reshape capital formation worldwide.

The Filing That Almost Destroyed the Company

Adrian Vega always believed building the technology would be the hardest part.

He was wrong. His company, Quantum Harbor Systems, developed advanced AI infrastructure protecting global financial institutions from cyberattacks. Over seven years, the business grew from a tiny startup in Tampa into one of the most respected cybersecurity firms in the industry. Major banks, insurance companies, and government agencies depended on Quantum Harbor software to monitor digital threats in real time.

Revenue exploded rapidly.

Investors pushed aggressively for a public listing.

Adrian initially focused almost entirely on valuation. Financial projections looked extraordinary. Private market demand remained strong. Analysts predicted Quantum Harbor could become one of the largest direct listings in cybersecurity history.

But Adrian underestimated one critical reality.

Going public was not only about growth.

It was about regulation.

The problems began during the SEC review process.

At first, everything appeared normal. Lawyers prepared registration statements, accountants finalized audited financials, and advisors coordinated exchange discussions. Adrian assumed the process would move smoothly because the company itself remained fundamentally strong.

Then the comment letters arrived.

The U.S. Securities and Exchange Commission requested additional disclosures regarding customer concentration risks, cybersecurity liabilities, revenue recognition policies, and international data privacy exposure.

The requests seemed manageable initially.

But each response triggered additional questions.

Weeks turned into months.

Adrian grew increasingly frustrated.

"We already explained this," he snapped during one legal meeting.

His lead securities attorney, Rebecca Lin, remained calm.

"They're not looking for short answers," she explained. "They want full transparency."

The deeper regulators examined Quantum Harbor's operations, the more weaknesses emerged internally.

Several accounting systems lacked sufficient documentation. Certain international contracts involved inconsistent revenue timing methods. Cybersecurity incident reporting procedures needed stronger oversight controls. Governance committees existed technically but lacked formal operating structures required for public-company compliance.

None of the problems appeared catastrophic individually.

Together, however, they threatened the entire listing timeline.

Pressure intensified rapidly.

Private investors wanted liquidity. Employees expected the public offering to move forward. Competitors prepared aggressively to exploit any signs of weakness. Financial media began questioning why the listing remained delayed.

Inside the company, morale started deteriorating.

Engineers complained about endless compliance meetings replacing product development focus. Finance teams worked around the clock rebuilding internal reporting systems.

Executives faced constant legal reviews regarding disclosure obligations.

Adrian became exhausted.

One evening around midnight, he sat alone in the office reviewing another set of regulatory revisions when Rebecca walked into the conference room carrying coffee.

“You look terrible,” she said.

Adrian laughed bitterly.

“I built an AI company,” he replied. “Now apparently I’m running a compliance company.”

Rebecca sat quietly across from him.

“This is the real transition,” she explained. “Private companies focus on growth. Public companies survive on trust.”

The words stayed with Adrian.

Over the following months, Quantum Harbor transformed internally.

Independent directors joined the board. Audit committees gained stronger oversight authority. Internal accounting systems were rebuilt completely. Cybersecurity disclosure protocols expanded dramatically. Executive training intensified regarding insider trading rules, earnings communication standards, and governance obligations.

At times, Adrian questioned whether going public remained worth the stress.

Then a major crisis struck. A competing cybersecurity company collapsed publicly after regulators discovered misleading disclosures involving customer retention metrics. The company's stock crashed nearly eighty percent within days. Lawsuits followed immediately. Executives resigned. Investors lost billions.

Financial markets panicked temporarily regarding cybersecurity listings generally.

Inside Quantum Harbor headquarters, fear spread rapidly.

Several executives suggested delaying the direct listing indefinitely.

But Rebecca disagreed.

"This is exactly why regulation matters," she said firmly. "Trust is everything now."

Adrian finally understood.

The compliance process was not designed to punish companies.

It existed to protect investor confidence.

Without trust, public markets could not function sustainably.

Determined to move forward correctly, Adrian doubled down on transparency. Instead of minimizing risks during filings, Quantum Harbor expanded disclosures aggressively. The company openly discussed cybersecurity threats, operational challenges, international regulatory exposure, and competitive risks in extraordinary detail.

Some advisors worried the disclosures sounded too cautious.

Adrian ignored them.

"If investors trust us," he said, "we'll be fine long term."

Months later, the SEC finally approved the registration.

The direct listing moved forward.

By then, Quantum Harbor looked completely different internally than it had a year earlier. Governance systems operated professionally. Financial controls met public-company standards. Executive accountability strengthened substantially. Compliance culture became deeply integrated throughout the organization.

The listing itself succeeded beyond expectations.

Institutional investors praised the company's transparency. Analysts highlighted the strength of governance systems. Retail investors appreciated management's honesty regarding operational risks instead of exaggerated hype. Most importantly, market confidence remained stable during periods of volatility because investors trusted leadership credibility.

Several months after the listing, Adrian spoke at a technology conference about the experience.

A young founder asked him what the hardest part of going public had been.

Adrian smiled thoughtfully before answering.

"Learning that public markets aren't built on valuations," he said. "They're built on trust."

The room became silent.

"Technology gets attention," he continued. "Growth creates excitement. But trust is what allows companies to survive once they become public."

Years later, Quantum Harbor became one of the most respected cybersecurity firms on the market, not because it avoided regulation, but because it embraced transparency and governance discipline earlier than most competitors.

And Adrian eventually realized something surprising:

The filing process that almost destroyed the company had actually saved it from becoming the type of public business investors eventually stop believing in.

Chapter 8

Building a Company That Is Ready for a Direct Listing

A successful direct listing begins long before a company ever files regulatory documents or appears on a public exchange. In reality, the process starts years earlier through the deliberate construction of a business capable of surviving and thriving under public market scrutiny. Many founders mistakenly believe a direct listing is primarily a financial transaction. While the listing itself is certainly a capital markets event, the true foundation of success lies in building an operationally disciplined, financially transparent, strategically scalable, and psychologically resilient organization.

Public markets expose weaknesses rapidly. Companies that enter public trading environments without strong internal systems, governance discipline, financial controls, leadership maturity, and strategic clarity often struggle regardless of how exciting their products or growth stories appear initially. Direct listings can create extraordinary opportunities for founders, employees, and investors, but they also remove many protective layers associated with private company operations. Once public, every decision, earnings report, leadership comment, operational challenge, and strategic mistake becomes visible to investors, analysts, competitors, regulators, and the media.

As a result, companies considering direct listings must focus heavily on readiness rather than simply timing. A business may possess strong revenue growth yet still lack the operational infrastructure required for sustainable public market success. True readiness involves much more than valuation. It involves building systems capable of supporting transparency, accountability, consistency, scalability, and long-term investor confidence.

One of the first requirements for direct listing readiness is financial maturity. Public market investors expect reliable, audited, transparent financial reporting supported by strong accounting systems and disciplined internal controls. Many startup companies initially prioritize growth speed over accounting sophistication during early development phases. While this approach may work privately for a time, public markets demand far higher levels of financial precision.

Companies preparing for direct listings must invest heavily in accounting infrastructure, financial reporting systems, budgeting processes, audit readiness, compliance controls, and forecasting capabilities. Revenue recognition practices must be consistent and defensible. Expense tracking systems must become highly organized. Cash flow management must remain transparent. Investors expect management teams to understand not only revenue growth but also profitability drivers, customer acquisition economics, retention metrics, operational leverage, and long-term margin potential.

Predictability becomes critically important in public markets. Investors reward businesses capable of producing consistent financial performance while communicating future expectations accurately. Companies with chaotic forecasting processes or inconsistent reporting structures often struggle after becoming public because investors lose confidence when surprises emerge unexpectedly.

Building strong internal controls is another essential component of readiness. Public companies operate under extensive regulatory oversight requiring accurate reporting and operational accountability. Internal control systems help prevent fraud, reduce reporting errors, monitor compliance obligations, and protect shareholder interests. Companies that postpone these systems until immediately before listing often encounter severe operational stress during the transition process.

Leadership maturity also becomes increasingly important as companies approach direct listings. Founders who excel at early-stage innovation are not always naturally prepared for the demands of public-company leadership. Running a public company requires balancing long-term strategic execution with short-term market expectations while communicating effectively with investors, regulators, analysts, employees, and media organizations simultaneously.

Public-company leadership demands emotional discipline. Market volatility, analyst criticism, shareholder activism, media pressure, and quarterly reporting cycles create intense psychological pressure. Founders must learn how to maintain strategic focus during periods of both euphoria and fear. Investors often evaluate leadership quality as closely as they evaluate financial metrics because management credibility heavily influences market confidence.

Executive teams must also evolve operationally. Public companies require experienced finance executives, legal counsel, investor relations professionals, compliance officers, cybersecurity specialists, governance advisors, and operational leaders capable of supporting complex reporting and communication obligations. Founders attempting to maintain overly centralized control structures may struggle under public market conditions.

Corporate governance readiness represents another critical factor. Investors increasingly expect companies to establish independent boards, audit committees, compensation oversight systems, governance frameworks, and ethical accountability structures before entering public markets. Strong governance signals professionalism, maturity, and shareholder alignment.

Board composition matters significantly. Public market investors often prefer boards containing individuals with operational expertise, financial knowledge, industry experience, regulatory familiarity, and governance credibility. Independent directors capable of challenging management constructively help strengthen investor confidence while improving long-term strategic oversight.

Company culture also plays an important role in public readiness. Organizations built entirely around short-term growth at all costs may struggle once public scrutiny intensifies. Sustainable public companies typically develop cultures emphasizing operational excellence, ethical behavior, accountability, adaptability, transparency, and disciplined execution.

Employees must also prepare psychologically for life inside a public company. Public listings can dramatically alter organizational dynamics. Stock price movements suddenly influence morale, employee conversations, media coverage, and personal financial expectations. Leadership teams must help employees maintain focus on long-term mission execution rather than becoming emotionally consumed by daily market fluctuations.

Scalability becomes another major consideration. Public market investors typically value companies based heavily on future growth potential rather than simply current performance. Businesses pursuing direct listings must demonstrate scalable operating models capable of supporting sustained expansion over many years. Investors look for repeatable revenue systems, efficient customer acquisition models, expanding margins, operational leverage, defensible competitive advantages, and growing market opportunities.

Technology infrastructure readiness is especially important for modern companies. Public businesses face heightened cybersecurity risks, data privacy obligations, operational continuity expectations, and disclosure responsibilities. Cybersecurity failures or technology outages can destroy market confidence rapidly. Companies pursuing direct listings must therefore strengthen technical infrastructure, security protocols, disaster recovery systems, and operational resilience significantly before entering public markets.

Investor communication readiness also becomes essential. Public companies must communicate consistently, transparently, and strategically with investors. Earnings calls, shareholder letters, media interviews, conference presentations, regulatory filings, and public statements all influence investor perception and valuation dynamics.

Founders often underestimate the importance of investor relations capabilities. Strong investor communication builds trust, reduces uncertainty, and strengthens long-term shareholder relationships. Weak communication increases confusion, volatility, speculation, and market anxiety. Companies preparing for direct listings should begin building investor communication systems long before the actual listing process begins.

Market positioning also influences direct listing readiness. Companies with strong brand recognition, customer loyalty, and public visibility often perform better during direct listings because investors already understand the business model and value proposition. Lesser-known businesses may struggle to generate sufficient market interest without extensive underwriting promotion.

This is one reason why many successful direct listings involve companies with broad consumer awareness or highly visible

media exposure, and strategic decision-making dynamics all evolve significantly. Preparing for these cultural and psychological shifts is just as important as preparing financial statements or regulatory filings.

The rise of direct listings reflects broader changes occurring throughout modern entrepreneurship and finance. Companies today possess greater flexibility regarding how they access public markets. However, flexibility does not eliminate the need for preparation. In many ways, direct listings demand even greater operational confidence because companies rely more heavily on market trust and less on underwriting stabilization mechanisms.

Ultimately, building a company ready for a direct listing means building a company ready for long-term public accountability. It requires creating systems capable of supporting transparency, governance, scalability, resilience, operational excellence, and investor confidence simultaneously.

The companies that succeed most consistently in public markets are rarely those with the loudest hype or most dramatic narratives. They are often the businesses that quietly spent years building strong foundations before ever ringing an exchange bell.

Public markets reward preparation.

And preparation begins long before the listing itself.

The Company That Waited Two Extra Years

When investors first pushed AtlasCore Technologies toward a public listing, founder Maya Sinclair felt tempted to move quickly.

The company's growth looked extraordinary.

AtlasCore had built one of the most advanced AI-driven logistics optimization platforms in the world. Major retailers, shipping companies, and manufacturing corporations relied on the software to predict supply chain disruptions and reduce operational costs. Revenue doubled repeatedly over several years while private market valuations surged beyond five billion dollars.

Venture capital firms wanted liquidity.

Employees dreamed about financial freedom.

Financial media called AtlasCore one of the hottest private technology companies in America.

Wall Street banks immediately began competing aggressively for the public offering.

At first, Maya assumed the company was ready.

Then she attended a dinner in New York with several founders who recently went public.

What she heard changed everything.

One founder described how his company collapsed operationally after becoming public because financial reporting systems could not handle quarterly disclosure requirements. Another explained how internal conflicts exploded after employees became obsessed with daily stock price movements. A third admitted his executive team lacked the emotional discipline necessary for constant analyst scrutiny and media pressure.

The stories disturbed Maya deeply.

On the flight home to Miami, she reviewed AtlasCore's internal operations honestly for the first time through the lens of public-market readiness rather than private-market growth.

The problems became obvious immediately.

Revenue growth remained strong, but forecasting systems lacked consistency. Financial controls varied across international divisions. Cybersecurity documentation remained incomplete. Governance committees technically existed but operated informally. Investor communication strategy barely existed at all. Operationally, the company still behaved like a startup.

Yet investors expected it to function like a mature public corporation.

The next morning, Maya gathered her executive team.

"We're not ready," she said directly.

The room became silent.

Several executives disagreed immediately.

The CFO argued market conditions looked favorable. Venture capital investors wanted liquidity soon. Competitors were scaling rapidly. Investment bankers warned the current valuation environment might not last forever.

But Maya refused to ignore reality.

"Going public doesn't fix weak systems," she said. "It exposes them."

Her decision shocked investors.

Instead of moving forward with an immediate direct listing, Maya delayed the process indefinitely and launched a complete operational transformation initiative internally.

The next two years became the hardest period in AtlasCore's history. At first, employees struggled to understand the decision. Some became frustrated watching other startups go public while AtlasCore remained private despite strong growth. Several investors pressured Maya aggressively to accelerate the timeline.

But Maya remained disciplined.

"We're building a company designed to survive public markets," she explained repeatedly. "Not just enter them."

The transformation touched every part of the business.

Financial systems were rebuilt entirely. Internal controls expanded dramatically. Independent auditors reviewed operational processes continuously. Governance committees gained stronger authority. Experienced public-company executives joined the leadership team. Cybersecurity infrastructure underwent extensive upgrades.

Maya also focused heavily on culture.

She worried employees might eventually become emotionally distracted by stock prices and short-term market sentiment after the listing. To prepare, leadership launched internal programs emphasizing long-term mission focus, operational excellence, and disciplined execution rather than valuation obsession. At times, the pressure became overwhelming. Competitors mocked AtlasCore publicly for delaying its listing. Financial journalists speculated the company lacked confidence. Venture investors warned Maya she risked missing ideal market conditions.

One board meeting became especially tense.

A major investor slammed his hand on the conference table.

“You’re costing everyone money by waiting,” he argued angrily.

Maya looked directly at him.

“No,” she replied calmly. “I’m protecting the company from becoming unstable after the listing.”

The room fell silent.

Months later, global markets entered a period of severe volatility.

Several rapidly rushed technology IPOs collapsed publicly after weak earnings, governance failures, cybersecurity incidents, and operational reporting problems emerged. Investors lost confidence in businesses that looked exciting privately but lacked the infrastructure necessary for public-company life.

Inside AtlasCore headquarters, employees watched the chaos carefully. Gradually, skepticism regarding Maya's decision disappeared.

By the second year of preparation, AtlasCore looked completely different operationally. Financial reporting became highly sophisticated. Governance systems operated professionally. Forecasting accuracy improved dramatically. Executive communication discipline strengthened substantially.

Most importantly, the company developed emotional maturity.

Leadership no longer chased hype cycles or short-term valuation excitement. Teams focused intensely on sustainable execution, customer retention, operational scalability, and long-term strategic growth.

Finally, after nearly two extra years of preparation, Maya believed AtlasCore was ready.

The company officially announced plans for a direct listing.

This time, investor reaction felt completely different.

Analysts praised the company's operational discipline. Institutional investors highlighted the strength of governance systems. Media coverage focused heavily on AtlasCore's preparation process rather than speculative hype. Even skeptical venture investors acknowledged the business appeared unusually mature compared to most high-growth technology companies entering public markets. On listing day, volatility remained manageable despite broader market uncertainty.

Investors trusted the company.

That trust changed everything.

Months later, while many newly public technology companies struggled with missed forecasts, governance controversies, and collapsing valuations, AtlasCore continued executing steadily. Revenue growth remained consistent. Employee morale stayed strong. Investor confidence deepened gradually over time.

One evening after quarterly earnings results exceeded expectations again, Maya walked through the company's headquarters quietly after most employees had gone home.

She stopped beside a framed photograph taken years earlier during the company's startup phase.

Tiny office.

Folding tables.

Secondhand laptops.

A handful of exhausted engineers chasing an impossible dream.

At that moment, Maya realized something important.

Most founders think going public is the destination.

But public markets are not the finish line.

They are the beginning of an entirely different level of accountability.

And the companies that survive public markets successfully are usually not the ones that moved fastest.

They are the ones that prepared longest.

Chapter 9

Liquidity, Founder Wealth, and Employee Equity in Direct Listings

One of the most powerful motivations behind direct listings is liquidity. While public market discussions often focus heavily on valuation, media attention, and market structure, the true human impact of public offerings frequently centers around the ability of founders, employees, and early investors to finally access the value they spent years building. Direct listings fundamentally reshape how liquidity events occur, how ownership transitions happen, and how wealth is distributed among stakeholders inside high-growth companies.

For many startup founders and employees, wealth exists primarily on paper for years before any liquidity event occurs. Equity ownership may carry enormous theoretical value while remaining completely illiquid in practical terms. Founders often sacrifice salaries, personal savings, relationships, stability, and years of intense pressure building companies that may eventually become highly valuable but provide little immediate financial security during early growth phases. Employees frequently accept below-market compensation in exchange for stock options or restricted equity because they believe in the long-term vision of the business.

A successful public listing can transform those illiquid ownership positions into real financial opportunity. Homes can be purchased. Debt can be eliminated. Families can be supported. Investments can be diversified. Generational wealth can be created. Entire lives may change financially within a matter of months.

Direct listings alter this process significantly compared to traditional IPOs because they prioritize market-driven liquidity rather than heavily controlled underwriting distribution systems. Understanding how liquidity works inside direct listings is therefore essential for founders, executives, employees, and investors seeking to maximize long-term wealth outcomes while maintaining strategic discipline.

In traditional IPOs, companies usually issue newly created shares to institutional investors through underwriting syndicates. Existing shareholders often face strict lock-up periods preventing them from selling shares for several months after the offering. These restrictions aim to reduce immediate selling pressure and stabilize stock prices during the early public trading period.

While lock-up periods may benefit short-term market stability, they can create frustration among founders and employees who waited years for liquidity opportunities. Many employees continue facing personal financial stress even after the company becomes public because they remain unable to access the value of their equity immediately.

Direct listings frequently provide greater flexibility regarding liquidity timing. Existing shareholders may be permitted to sell shares directly into the public market once trading begins, often without the same restrictive lock-up structures associated with traditional IPOs. This creates important advantages for employees, founders, and early investors seeking earlier access to liquidity.

However, this flexibility also introduces strategic complexity.

Liquidity itself is emotionally powerful. When individuals suddenly gain access to life-changing wealth, emotional decision-making can become dangerous. Employees who never previously managed large amounts of money may feel overwhelming pressure to sell immediately. Founders may struggle balancing personal financial security against long-term ownership conviction. Early investors may debate whether to exit aggressively or maintain exposure to future upside.

Direct listings therefore require not only financial planning but also psychological discipline. For founders, one of the biggest wealth-related decisions involves ownership concentration. Many entrepreneurs spend years with the majority of their net worth tied almost entirely to a single private company. While concentrated ownership can create enormous upside during growth phases, it also creates substantial risk. A public listing introduces opportunities for diversification that may significantly reduce personal financial vulnerability.

Yet diversification itself can create difficult emotional conflicts.

Founders who sell too aggressively immediately after listing may signal reduced confidence to the market. Investors often monitor insider selling behavior closely. Heavy founder liquidation can damage market perception even when motivated by reasonable diversification goals rather than pessimism regarding the company's future.

Balancing these dynamics requires careful strategy.

Some founders choose gradual diversification approaches over many years rather than immediate large-scale selling. Others maintain significant long-term ownership positions while slowly reducing concentration risk through structured financial planning. Wealth preservation becomes increasingly important once companies reach public market scale because protecting wealth often becomes more important than maximizing additional upside aggressively. Employees face similar challenges. Many startup employees underestimate the complexity of equity compensation and liquidity planning. Stock options, restricted stock units, vesting schedules, tax obligations, exercise timing, alternative minimum tax exposure, capital gains treatment, and diversification strategy all become critically important once liquidity arrives.

Without proper planning, employees may make emotionally driven decisions that create unnecessary tax liabilities or long-term financial mistakes. Some individuals sell too quickly out of fear. Others hold excessively concentrated positions because of emotional attachment to the company. Both extremes can create problems.

Financial education therefore becomes extremely valuable before direct listings occur. Companies that help employees understand taxation, diversification, financial planning, and liquidity management often support healthier long-term outcomes for their workforce. Employees suddenly transitioning from modest salaries to multimillion-dollar net worth positions may experience enormous psychological and financial stress if unprepared.

Early investors also play major roles in direct listing liquidity dynamics. Venture capital firms, angel investors, private equity groups, and early backers often invested years before the public listing occurred. Some funds may face pressure from limited partners to realize returns and distribute capital. Others may remain highly optimistic regarding future growth potential.

The timing and scale of investor selling activity influence market psychology significantly. Public investors closely analyze insider transactions searching for signals regarding confidence and future expectations. Healthy liquidity distribution generally involves balanced selling behavior rather than aggressive mass liquidation immediately after listing.

One of the most important advantages of direct listings is the potential reduction of dilution. Traditional IPOs commonly issue substantial new shares to raise additional capital, increasing the total share count and reducing existing ownership percentages. Direct listings often focus more heavily on secondary sales involving existing shares rather than massive primary issuance.

For founders and employees, preserving ownership percentages can dramatically impact long-term wealth creation. Even small differences in dilution become extremely meaningful as companies scale over time. Retaining greater ownership allows founders and employees to participate more fully in future value appreciation.

Control also becomes an important consideration. Founders often worry not only about wealth creation but also about maintaining strategic influence after becoming public companies. Ownership dilution can weaken voting power, governance influence, and long-term operational control. Some founders structure ownership carefully to preserve decision-making authority even after public listings occur.

Dual-class share structures sometimes support these objectives by granting founders enhanced voting rights relative to public shareholders. While controversial among certain investors, these structures allow founders to maintain long-term strategic vision without excessive short-term market pressure.

Another major liquidity-related issue involves secondary markets before direct listings occur. Many private companies now allow limited secondary transactions before public offerings, enabling employees and early investors to sell portions of their holdings privately. These markets create earlier liquidity opportunities while helping establish reference valuations before public trading begins.

However, secondary markets also create complexities regarding pricing expectations, shareholder composition, and public market psychology. If private secondary valuations become excessively inflated before public listings, investors may react negatively if public trading fails to support those expectations.

The relationship between liquidity and company culture also deserves careful attention.

Sudden wealth changes organizational psychology dramatically. Employees who become financially independent may change career priorities, work motivation, risk tolerance, or lifestyle expectations. Some leave immediately after liquidity events. Others become less focused operationally because financial pressure disappears.

Strong leadership teams prepare for these transitions proactively. Companies that maintain mission-driven cultures while supporting healthy employee wealth outcomes often navigate liquidity events more successfully than organizations unprepared for the psychological effects of sudden financial change.

Public market investors also evaluate liquidity structures strategically. Investors generally prefer orderly liquidity transitions rather than chaotic insider selling behavior.

Companies demonstrating thoughtful planning around shareholder liquidity often build stronger market confidence.

Founders pursuing direct listings must therefore communicate liquidity expectations carefully. Transparency regarding shareholder intentions, ownership structures, insider sales policies, and long-term strategic alignment reduces uncertainty while strengthening investor trust.

Tax planning becomes another major component of liquidity management.

Public equity sales can trigger substantial tax obligations depending on holding periods, compensation structures, jurisdictional rules, and transaction timing. Founders and employees who fail to plan proactively may face unexpected liabilities that significantly reduce net wealth outcomes.

Many wealthy founders eventually build sophisticated long-term wealth management structures involving trusts, family offices, philanthropic vehicles, tax planning entities, diversified investment portfolios, and estate planning systems. Liquidity events often become the starting point for entirely new phases of financial strategy focused on preservation, diversification, and generational wealth creation.

The emotional dimension of wealth creation should not be underestimated either.

Many founders spend years emotionally identifying themselves with their companies. Selling shares can feel psychologically uncomfortable because ownership becomes tied closely to identity, purpose, and personal sacrifice. Some founders struggle emotionally after liquidity events because they spent so long pursuing financial milestones without preparing psychologically for life afterward. Employees experience similar emotional transitions. Financial independence may solve certain problems while creating entirely new questions regarding purpose, ambition, identity, and long-term fulfillment.

This is why some of the most successful founders emphasize mission and long-term vision even after achieving extraordinary wealth. Sustainable fulfillment rarely comes solely from liquidity itself. Meaningful work, strategic challenge, impact, creativity, and personal growth continue mattering long after financial security arrives.

The evolution of direct listings reflects broader changes occurring throughout entrepreneurship and capital markets. Modern founders increasingly seek liquidity pathways that preserve ownership, reduce unnecessary dilution, improve fairness, and align more closely with long-term strategic goals. Employees increasingly expect equity participation as meaningful components of compensation and wealth creation.

Public markets are no longer simply mechanisms for raising capital. They are wealth distribution systems capable of transforming the lives of thousands of stakeholders connected to growing companies.

Ultimately, liquidity represents more than financial access. It represents freedom, opportunity, security, flexibility, and the realization of years of sacrifice and risk-taking. Founders who understand how to manage liquidity intelligently position themselves not only for successful public offerings, but also for sustainable long-term wealth creation after the listing occurs.

The Employee Who Almost Sold Everything

When HorizonGrid AI announced its direct listing, employees throughout the company erupted with excitement.

For nearly nine years, the business operated privately while building one of the world's fastest-growing artificial intelligence infrastructure platforms. What started as a tiny machine learning startup in Orlando evolved into a global software powerhouse serving major corporations, logistics networks, and financial institutions.

Inside the company, stock options became legendary.

Early employees joked constantly about becoming "paper millionaires," but after years without liquidity, most of the wealth remained theoretical. Some employees borrowed money while holding valuable stock options they could not access. Others delayed major life decisions waiting for the company to eventually go public.

Then the announcement finally came.

HorizonGrid would pursue a direct listing.

No traditional IPO.

No long lock-up periods.

Employees could potentially sell shares immediately once public trading began.

Excitement spread instantly through every department.

One employee felt the emotional pressure more intensely than almost anyone else.

David Morales joined HorizonGrid during its earliest days as a junior software engineer earning a modest salary far below industry standards. At the time, the company operated out of a cramped office with folding chairs, unreliable internet, and constant funding uncertainty.

Most people thought the company would fail.

David stayed anyway.

Over the years, his stock options accumulated gradually while the company's valuation exploded privately. By the time the direct listing announcement occurred, his equity position had become worth millions of dollars on paper.

But David's personal life remained complicated. His parents still lived in a small apartment in Tampa struggling financially. His younger sister carried heavy student debt. David himself rented a modest condo and drove an aging car despite technically being wealthy on paper.

Now, suddenly, everything was about to change.

In the weeks before the listing, employees talked constantly about potential stock prices, wealth projections, and financial freedom. Some planned to buy luxury homes immediately. Others discussed early retirement, exotic vacations, or launching investment portfolios.

David became emotionally overwhelmed.

He had never managed significant wealth before. The idea of becoming financially independent felt surreal.

Then fear entered the picture.

Financial media coverage surrounding the direct listing became increasingly volatile. Analysts debated whether AI valuations were sustainable. Commentators warned about market instability. Several recently public technology companies experienced severe stock declines shortly after listing.

David panicked internally.

"What if the stock crashes?" he wondered constantly. The fear intensified daily.

A week before the listing, David made a decision privately.

He planned to sell almost everything immediately after trading began.

The idea comforted him psychologically. Selling would eliminate uncertainty completely. He could pay off family debt, buy a house, invest conservatively, and never worry financially again.

But he told nobody.

Meanwhile, HorizonGrid's founder and CEO, Rachel Kim, recognized growing emotional tension across the company. Employees who spent years focused purely on building products now obsessed constantly over stock prices and future wealth.

Rachel understood the danger.

One afternoon, she organized an internal meeting focused entirely on financial education and long-term wealth planning. Independent advisors explained diversification strategy, tax planning, concentrated equity risk, emotional decision-making, and the psychological impact of sudden liquidity.

David listened carefully but remained unconvinced.

Then one advisor said something unexpected.

"The biggest financial mistake many employees make after liquidity events," he explained, "is making permanent decisions based on temporary emotions."

The sentence stayed in David's mind.

After the presentation ended, David approached the advisor privately.

"I'm thinking about selling everything immediately," he admitted.

The advisor nodded calmly.

"That's common."

"Is it a bad idea?"

The advisor smiled slightly.

"That depends. Are you making the decision strategically or emotionally?"

David did not answer immediately.

That night, he sat alone in his condo reviewing HorizonGrid's long-term financial projections. He remembered the company's early struggles, the product breakthroughs, the customer growth, and the enormous market opportunity still ahead. Deep down, he still believed in the business strongly.

But fear kept pushing him toward safety.

Listing day arrived.

As HorizonGrid shares began trading publicly, volatility exploded immediately. Financial television networks covered every price movement obsessively. Social media filled with emotional reactions ranging from euphoric optimism to panic.

The stock surged aggressively during the opening hours.

David stared at the trading screen anxiously.

His account value climbed beyond anything he previously imagined possible.

Then suddenly, the stock dropped sharply.

Fear hit him instantly.

Without thinking carefully, David logged into his brokerage account and prepared to sell nearly his entire position.

His finger hovered over the confirmation button.

Then his phone rang.

It was Rachel. “I figured you might be stressed today,” she said calmly.

David laughed nervously.

“That obvious?”

Rachel paused briefly.

"Look," she said, "I'm not telling anyone what to do with their shares. Everyone has different financial situations. But don't let short-term volatility make long-term decisions for you."

David stared silently at the screen.

"The market is emotional today," Rachel continued. "That doesn't mean the company suddenly changed."

After the call ended, David sat quietly for nearly an hour thinking.

Finally, he adjusted his strategy completely.

Instead of selling everything, he sold only enough shares to eliminate personal debt, help his parents financially, and create basic financial security. He kept the majority of his ownership position invested long term while gradually diversifying over time.

That decision changed his life permanently.

Over the following years, HorizonGrid continued growing aggressively as artificial intelligence transformed global industries. The stock price experienced volatility constantly, but long-term value creation remained extraordinary.

Because David maintained meaningful ownership, his wealth expanded far beyond what he initially expected.

More importantly, he learned an even greater lesson.

Liquidity creates opportunity.

But emotional discipline determines whether wealth lasts.

Years later, David became one of HorizonGrid's senior engineering executives while mentoring younger employees preparing for their own future liquidity events.

Whenever employees asked him for financial advice, he always repeated the same sentence:

"Don't let temporary fear make permanent decisions for your future."

Because he came very close to doing exactly that himself.

Chapter 10

The Future of Direct Listings and the Evolution of Public Markets

The world of capital markets is entering one of the most transformative periods in financial history. For generations, public offerings followed relatively predictable structures dominated by large investment banks, institutional investors, centralized exchanges, and traditional underwriting systems. Companies seeking public capital generally followed the same path: private growth, venture financing, institutional roadshows, IPO pricing negotiations, and eventual stock exchange listings managed through established Wall Street frameworks.

Today, however, that system is evolving rapidly.

Direct listings represent far more than a temporary financial trend or alternative transaction structure. They symbolize a broader shift in how businesses, investors, and entrepreneurs think about ownership, liquidity, transparency, control, and access to capital. As technology advances, private capital markets expand, retail investing grows, decentralized finance develops, and global communication accelerates, the future of public markets may look dramatically different from the systems that dominated previous decades.

Understanding the future of direct listings requires understanding the deeper forces reshaping global finance itself.

One of the most important changes involves the democratization of information. Historically, institutional investors possessed significant informational advantages compared to retail investors. Large banks, hedge funds, and private financial networks controlled much of the market intelligence surrounding private companies and public offerings. Today, digital platforms, financial media, social networks, AI-driven analytics, and open-access information systems allow investors worldwide to analyze businesses more independently than ever before.

This shift weakens some of the traditional gatekeeping advantages previously held by underwriting institutions. Companies with strong brands, transparent operations, loyal customer bases, and global visibility can now communicate directly with investors at unprecedented scale. Direct listings align naturally with this environment because they emphasize market-driven participation rather than heavily centralized allocation systems.

Technology companies in particular may continue leading this transition because they often possess large user communities, global brand recognition, and digital-native communication capabilities long before entering public markets. Businesses built around platforms, software ecosystems, artificial intelligence, fintech, creator economies, and online marketplaces may increasingly question whether traditional IPO structures remain necessary under all circumstances.

Another major trend shaping the future involves the expansion of private capital availability. Venture capital firms, sovereign wealth funds, family offices, growth equity funds, private equity firms, and secondary market platforms now provide companies with access to enormous amounts of private funding. As a result, many businesses remain private much longer than previous generations while achieving valuations once associated only with public corporations.

This changes the purpose of public offerings themselves.

Historically, companies often pursued IPOs primarily because they needed large amounts of growth capital unavailable elsewhere. Increasingly, modern companies may pursue public listings more for liquidity, visibility, acquisition currency, and strategic positioning rather than urgent fundraising needs. Direct listings align especially well with businesses already possessing strong balance sheets and sufficient private capital access. The rise of secondary markets also contributes to this evolution. Employees, founders, and early investors increasingly access liquidity before public listings through private secondary transactions. This reduces pressure to rush into traditional IPOs simply to create shareholder liquidity. Over time, public market transitions may become more strategic and less financially urgent.

Another powerful force shaping future direct listings is the growth of retail investor participation. Digital brokerage platforms, commission-free trading, financial education content, and online investing communities have dramatically increased retail involvement in financial markets. Millions of individuals now participate directly in stock investing, options trading, cryptocurrency markets, and alternative asset ecosystems.

Many retail investors view direct listings positively because they perceive them as fairer than traditional IPO allocation systems that heavily favor institutional investors. The demand for broader participation, transparency, and equal market access may continue pushing capital markets toward more open structures over time.

The psychology of younger generations also matters significantly. Younger entrepreneurs and investors often prioritize decentralization, transparency, flexibility, technology integration, and reduced institutional gatekeeping. These cultural attitudes align naturally with many principles underlying direct listings and alternative capital formation systems.

Blockchain technology and decentralized finance may further accelerate these trends.

Although still developing, blockchain infrastructure introduces the possibility of tokenized securities, decentralized ownership records, programmable financial contracts, and globally accessible liquidity systems operating with greater transparency and efficiency. Future public offerings may eventually integrate blockchain-based settlement systems, tokenized equity structures, or decentralized shareholder participation frameworks.

Some entrepreneurs already envision futures where companies raise capital globally through hybrid systems blending traditional securities regulation with blockchain-enabled ownership mechanisms. While regulatory complexity remains substantial, financial innovation continues accelerating rapidly.

Artificial intelligence will likely reshape public markets as well. AI-driven analytics systems increasingly evaluate companies, forecast financial trends, analyze investor sentiment, detect market anomalies, and automate portions of financial research. Investors may eventually rely heavily on AI systems capable of evaluating public companies in real time using enormous data sets impossible for humans to process manually.

This could influence how public offerings are priced, how investor demand develops, and how market perception evolves after listings occur. Companies capable of communicating clearly within AI-driven financial ecosystems may gain strategic advantages.

Globalization will also continue influencing capital market evolution. Businesses increasingly operate internationally from early stages of growth. Public market access may become more global, interconnected, and competitive as exchanges, investors, and financial platforms expand beyond traditional geographic limitations.

Cross-border direct listings, multinational liquidity structures, and international investor participation may become increasingly common. Companies may eventually evaluate multiple global exchanges strategically depending on investor demographics, industry specialization, regulatory frameworks, and liquidity conditions.

At the same time, regulation will continue evolving alongside innovation. Financial regulators face difficult balancing challenges. On one hand, they must support innovation, market efficiency, and capital formation. On the other hand, they must protect investors, maintain market integrity, reduce fraud risk, and preserve systemic stability.

The future regulatory environment surrounding direct listings, decentralized finance, digital securities, and alternative public offerings will likely remain highly dynamic. Companies operating within these evolving systems must remain adaptable and proactive regarding compliance expectations.

Corporate governance may evolve significantly as well.

Public investors increasingly focus on long-term strategic alignment, ESG factors, leadership quality, cybersecurity resilience, diversity initiatives, ethical behavior, and operational transparency. Future public companies may face even higher expectations regarding accountability and stakeholder responsibility.

Founders who understand governance strategically rather than viewing it merely as a compliance burden may build stronger investor relationships long term. Public trust will likely remain one of the most valuable assets any company can possess regardless of how capital markets evolve technologically.

The role of investment banks will also continue changing rather than disappearing entirely. Traditional underwriting institutions still provide substantial value involving market expertise, institutional relationships, research coverage, legal coordination, regulatory guidance, and strategic advisory capabilities. However, their role may shift increasingly toward advisory partnership rather than centralized control over the entire public offering process.

Hybrid models may become especially common.

Future companies may combine elements of direct listings, traditional IPOs, secondary offerings, decentralized financial tools, auction-based pricing systems, and strategic private placements into customized capital market strategies tailored to specific business needs. Financial flexibility will likely continue expanding.

Founder expectations are evolving too.

Modern entrepreneurs increasingly prioritize ownership preservation, long-term strategic control, operational independence, and aligned shareholder structures. Many founders now understand that how a company goes public can influence control dynamics, dilution levels, governance flexibility, employee incentives, and long-term wealth creation for decades afterward. This growing financial sophistication among founders may continue driving experimentation with alternative public offering models.

However, despite all these technological and structural changes, several timeless truths about public markets will likely remain unchanged.

Businesses will still need to create real value.

Leadership credibility will still matter enormously.

Operational execution will still determine long-term success.

Investor trust will still drive valuation stability.

Transparency will still support market confidence.

Psychology will still influence market behavior.

And sustainable wealth creation will still depend more heavily on long-term discipline than short-term hype.

One of the greatest risks during periods of financial innovation is confusing structural novelty with actual business quality. Investors and founders alike must remember that alternative public offering structures do not magically eliminate operational challenges, competitive pressures, market cycles, or strategic execution requirements.

The companies that succeed most consistently in future public markets will likely combine technological adaptability with operational fundamentals. They will embrace innovation without abandoning discipline. They will leverage new financial structures strategically while maintaining strong governance, transparency, and execution quality.

Direct listings themselves may also continue evolving. Regulatory changes may expand fundraising flexibility further. Exchanges may introduce additional mechanisms supporting liquidity and price discovery. Technology may improve transparency, settlement efficiency, and shareholder participation capabilities.

As more successful direct listings occur, investor comfort and institutional participation will likely strengthen gradually. What once seemed experimental may eventually become normalized within broader capital market ecosystems.

The future of public markets may ultimately become more decentralized, transparent, globally accessible, technology-driven, and founder-influenced than previous generations imagined possible.

For entrepreneurs, this creates extraordinary opportunity.

Founders entering business today possess access to tools, capital systems, communication channels, and financial flexibility unavailable at any other point in history. The ability to build, scale, finance, and publicly list companies has never been more accessible globally.

However, greater opportunity also creates greater responsibility.

Financial literacy becomes increasingly important. Founders who understand ownership structures, liquidity planning, governance systems, investor psychology, regulatory frameworks, and capital markets strategy will possess enormous advantages over entrepreneurs focused solely on products or growth metrics.

The next generation of iconic public companies may not emerge through identical pathways. Some will pursue traditional IPOs successfully. Others will leverage direct listings, decentralized financial systems, hybrid capital structures, or entirely new models not yet fully developed.

The future will reward adaptability.

Ultimately, direct listings represent more than financial innovation. They represent a broader philosophical shift toward flexibility, transparency, founder empowerment, and market-driven participation. They challenge assumptions regarding who controls public offerings, how liquidity should function, and how ownership should transition from private to public markets. As financial systems continue evolving, the entrepreneurs who understand these changes early will position themselves to create not only successful companies, but also long-term strategic wealth capable of lasting across generations.

The future of public markets is still being written.

And many of the founders reading about these systems today may eventually become the entrepreneurs shaping what those markets look like tomorrow.

The Founder Who Saw the Future Before Wall Street Did

In 2032, most of Wall Street still believed traditional IPOs would remain the dominant path into public markets forever.

Lucas Mercer disagreed completely.

His company, SynapseGrid Global, had become one of the fastest-growing AI infrastructure businesses in the world. The platform connected decentralized computing systems across international networks, allowing businesses to process massive

AI workloads without relying entirely on centralized cloud providers.

The company grew explosively.

Governments used the technology. Fortune 500 companies depended on it.

Investors valued SynapseGrid privately at nearly twenty-five billion dollars.

Naturally, major investment banks began aggressively pursuing the public offering.

Executives from New York, London, Hong Kong, and Dubai flew constantly to meet Lucas. They pitched traditional IPO structures worth hundreds of millions in underwriting fees. They promised institutional demand, analyst coverage, and global market prestige.

But Lucas had spent years studying the evolution of financial systems.

And he believed Wall Street was underestimating how quickly public markets were changing.

"We're still using twentieth-century structures for twenty-first-century companies," he told his executive team repeatedly.

Most people thought he sounded overly ambitious.

Even inside SynapseGrid, several board members worried Lucas had become too obsessed with financial innovation. Some investors argued the safest option remained a conventional IPO supported by established underwriting institutions.

But Lucas saw patterns others ignored.

Retail investing had exploded globally.

Blockchain settlement systems were becoming increasingly sophisticated.

AI-driven financial analysis reduced dependence on traditional institutional research.

Digital investor communities influenced market psychology faster than television networks ever could.

Private capital markets had already transformed how startups scaled.

To Lucas, direct listings represented only the beginning.

He envisioned an entirely new future for public markets.

Instead of relying heavily on centralized underwriting systems, Lucas wanted SynapseGrid's public transition to operate through a hybrid structure combining direct listing mechanics, blockchain-based shareholder verification, AI-driven investor transparency tools, and globally accessible trading systems.

Most bankers hated the idea immediately.

"That structure is too unconventional," one senior executive warned him. Lucas smiled calmly.

"Every important financial innovation sounded unconventional at first."

The debate intensified for nearly a year.

Regulators demanded extensive reviews. Legal teams worked around the clock. Financial media mocked the proposal constantly. Some analysts predicted disaster if SynapseGrid bypassed traditional underwriting structures too aggressively.

But younger investors reacted differently.

Online investing communities became fascinated by the company's vision. Technology entrepreneurs praised the transparency approach. International investors appreciated the accessibility. Retail participation interest surged globally.

Meanwhile, traditional Wall Street institutions grew increasingly nervous.

The real fear was not whether SynapseGrid's listing would fail.

The real fear was what would happen if it succeeded.

Because if Lucas proved companies could enter public markets successfully through more decentralized, transparent, technology-driven systems, it could permanently change the balance of power inside global finance. Inside SynapseGrid headquarters, employees sensed history unfolding.

One evening, Lucas gathered the senior leadership team inside the company's Miami operations center overlooking Biscayne Bay.

Massive digital screens displayed real-time investor participation data from around the world.

"This isn't just about our company," Lucas explained quietly. "This is about where public markets are heading."

Several executives looked uncertain.

"What if the market rejects it?" one asked.

Lucas paused thoughtfully.

"Then we adapt. But if we never evolve financial systems, innovation eventually stalls."

The final regulatory approvals arrived six months later.

Global media coverage exploded instantly.

Financial networks called SynapseGrid's public transition "the most important capital markets experiment of the decade." Critics warned about volatility risks, regulatory uncertainty, and institutional resistance. Supporters called it the beginning of a new era in finance. Listing day became one of the most closely watched events in market history.

Unlike traditional IPOs, investors worldwide participated simultaneously through integrated global trading systems. AI-driven analytics platforms provided real-time transparency regarding liquidity flows, shareholder participation, and pricing dynamics. Blockchain-based settlement systems verified ownership transfers almost instantly.

Volatility remained intense early.

Traditional institutional traders initially hesitated. Some hedge funds shorted the stock aggressively expecting failure. Financial commentators predicted chaos throughout the opening hours.

Then something unexpected happened.

The market stabilized remarkably quickly.

Investor participation broadened globally beyond what analysts predicted. Retail investors, international funds, technology-focused institutions, and decentralized investment groups all entered the market simultaneously. Liquidity remained strong. Transparency reduced uncertainty. Confidence gradually strengthened.

By the end of the first week, SynapseGrid became one of the most successful public market debuts in modern financial history. But the real impact came afterward.

Within two years, multiple global exchanges introduced new hybrid listing frameworks inspired partly by SynapseGrid's model. Regulators accelerated modernization initiatives. Investment banks shifted increasingly toward advisory-focused roles rather than centralized underwriting control.

Public markets began evolving faster than ever before.

Years later, during an interview at an international financial summit, a journalist asked Lucas whether he intentionally tried to disrupt Wall Street.

Lucas smiled slightly before answering.

"No," he said. "I simply believed public markets should evolve at the same speed as the companies entering them."

The room became silent.

"Technology changed communication. It changed commerce. It changed investing. Eventually, it had to change how companies go public too."

By then, Lucas was no longer viewed merely as a successful founder.

He was viewed as one of the entrepreneurs who helped accelerate the modernization of global capital markets themselves.

And the systems Wall Street once considered impossible had already begun becoming normal.

Final IPO Thoughts

The evolution of public markets continues accelerating faster than most people realize. What once seemed like a rigid financial system dominated entirely by traditional underwriting structures has transformed into a far more flexible and innovative landscape where founders, investors, employees, and companies now possess multiple pathways toward liquidity, capital formation, and long-term wealth creation. Direct listings represent one of the most important developments within this transformation because they challenge long-standing assumptions about how businesses should enter public markets and who should ultimately benefit from those transitions.

Throughout this book, one central theme has appeared repeatedly: public offerings are not simply financial transactions. They are strategic, psychological, operational, and life-changing events capable of reshaping ownership structures, personal wealth, employee futures, investor relationships, corporate governance, and long-term company trajectories. The way a business enters public markets can influence everything from founder control and shareholder dilution to market perception and organizational culture. Direct listings emerged because many modern founders began questioning whether traditional IPO systems always aligned with the best interests of companies and long-term shareholders. Entrepreneurs noticed situations where companies spent years creating value only to watch enormous portions of that value transfer quickly through underpriced offerings, restrictive lock-up structures, and highly controlled institutional allocation systems. They saw opportunities to create more transparent, flexible, and market-driven alternatives.

Yet this book has also demonstrated that direct listings are not magical shortcuts or universally superior solutions. They are tools. Like all financial tools, their effectiveness depends entirely on how, when, and why they are used. Some businesses remain excellent candidates for traditional IPOs because they require large capital raises, institutional support, market stabilization, or extensive analyst coverage. Other companies may benefit significantly from direct listings because they already possess strong brand recognition, operational maturity, healthy balance sheets, and substantial investor demand.

The most successful founders avoid ideological thinking when evaluating capital market strategies. They do not blindly follow trends. Instead, they analyze alignment. They ask whether the structure matches the company's financial position, shareholder goals, growth trajectory, liquidity needs, governance philosophy, and long-term strategic vision. They recognize that public market decisions are deeply contextual and should reflect the unique realities of the business rather than external hype or media excitement.

One of the greatest lessons within modern public markets is that flexibility creates power. Founders today possess more options than previous generations ever imagined possible. Traditional IPOs, direct listings, SPAC transactions, hybrid offerings, secondary liquidity programs, decentralized financial systems, and emerging blockchain-based capital formation tools continue expanding the strategic possibilities available to entrepreneurs worldwide. This evolution is reducing dependence on rigid gatekeeping systems while increasing founder influence over how companies transition into public ownership.

At the same time, the rise of alternative public offerings does not eliminate the importance of preparation, discipline, transparency, or operational excellence. In many ways, direct listings demand even greater confidence in the underlying business because companies rely more heavily on market trust and less on traditional underwriting structures designed to manage investor psychology artificially.

This is why readiness remains one of the most important concepts in the entire public listing process. Companies that enter public markets before developing strong governance systems, financial controls, leadership maturity, compliance infrastructure, communication discipline, and operational scalability often struggle regardless of valuation or hype. Public markets expose weaknesses rapidly. Businesses capable of sustaining long-term investor confidence usually spent years quietly strengthening foundations before ever appearing on an exchange.

Trust ultimately becomes the currency that matters most in public markets. Investors allocate capital toward businesses they believe are credible, transparent, disciplined, adaptable, and strategically competent. Leadership integrity matters enormously. Communication consistency matters enormously. Governance quality matters enormously. Financial accuracy matters enormously. Companies capable of building and maintaining trust frequently outperform businesses driven primarily by short-term speculation or marketing excitement.

This book also explored the emotional and psychological dimensions of public offerings because wealth creation itself is deeply emotional. Founders spend years sacrificing comfort, stability, and security while building businesses under enormous pressure. Employees often dedicate substantial portions of their lives to companies long before any liquidity exists. Investors commit capital and confidence into uncertain futures hoping that extraordinary growth eventually materializes.

When liquidity finally arrives, emotional discipline becomes just as important as financial intelligence.

Many founders discover that going public creates new pressures rather than eliminating old ones. Market volatility, analyst expectations, shareholder scrutiny, media attention, and governance responsibilities replace many of the earlier startup struggles. Public ownership introduces accountability at an entirely different scale. Founders who once operated privately now lead organizations under constant observation.

This transition requires psychological maturity.

Public markets reward leaders capable of remaining calm during periods of uncertainty while maintaining long-term strategic focus. Emotional overreaction, short-term decision-making, inconsistent communication, or loss of operational discipline can damage investor confidence quickly. The founders who succeed most consistently after public listings are often those who understand that wealth preservation and sustainable execution matter more long term than temporary valuation spikes or market hype. Employee

Operational discipline will remain essential.

Leadership credibility will remain essential.

Long-term strategic thinking will remain essential.

Public markets may evolve structurally, but human psychology and investor behavior will continue influencing outcomes fundamentally.

One of the most important realizations for founders is that becoming public is not the ultimate destination. It is a transition point. The listing event itself may generate enormous attention temporarily, but sustainable wealth creation depends far more on what happens afterward. Public markets reward businesses capable of executing consistently over many years while adapting intelligently to changing economic conditions, technological shifts, competitive pressures, and investor expectations.

Many founders spend years dreaming about ringing the exchange bell without fully understanding what comes next. The companies that thrive publicly usually approach the listing not as an ending, but as the beginning of an entirely new operational phase requiring even greater discipline, maturity, and strategic patience.

The rise of direct listings ultimately reflects something larger than finance itself. It reflects the growing desire for fairness, flexibility, transparency, and founder empowerment within modern entrepreneurship. It represents a broader shift toward systems that allow businesses to align capital market strategies more closely with long-term missions rather than blindly following historical conventions.

This does not mean traditional IPOs are obsolete. Far from it. Traditional underwriting structures continue providing meaningful value for many companies. But founders now possess choice. And choice changes everything.

Entrepreneurs who understand multiple pathways can negotiate from stronger positions. They can structure liquidity more intelligently. They can protect ownership more carefully. They can align public market transitions more closely with the interests of employees, investors, and long-term strategic objectives.

Knowledge creates leverage.

Throughout history, some of the greatest fortunes were created not simply by building businesses, but by understanding capital markets deeply. Founders who master how ownership, liquidity, governance, valuation, investor psychology, and market structure interact gain enormous advantages over competitors who focus solely on products or revenue growth.

This is why financial literacy matters so much for entrepreneurs. A founder may build an extraordinary business operationally yet still lose substantial ownership, control, or long-term wealth through poorly structured public transactions. Conversely, founders who understand capital markets strategically can preserve ownership, reduce dilution, maximize liquidity efficiency, and create generational wealth opportunities not only for themselves, but also for employees and shareholders.

The future belongs increasingly to founders capable of combining operational excellence with financial sophistication.

Direct listings are part of that future.

They symbolize a changing world where entrepreneurs no longer accept rigid systems automatically simply because "that's how it has always been done." They represent the growing realization that innovation should apply not only to products and technology, but also to capital formation, ownership distribution, and wealth creation itself.

As you finish this book, remember that every public offering structure ultimately exists for one purpose: transforming private value into public opportunity. The methods may evolve, but the core mission remains the same. Companies create value, markets allocate capital, and ownership creates wealth.

The founders who understand these systems deeply will shape the next generation of global businesses.

They will build companies differently.

They will approach ownership differently.

They will approach liquidity differently.

And they will likely redefine the future of public markets themselves.

The next era of capital markets has already begun.

The question is not whether financial systems will continue evolving.

The question is whether founders, investors, and entrepreneurs will prepare themselves early enough to benefit from that evolution intelligently.

www.ingramcontent.com/pod-product-compliance
Lightning Source LLC
LaVergne TN
LVHW040518210926
848480LV00007BA/1502